C0-FSF-311

THE NECESSARY ILLUSION

67
37
76

THE NECESSARY ILLUSION

CHURCH CULTURE AND EDUCATIONAL CHANGE

MALCOLM L. WARFORD

A PILGRIM PRESS BOOK
FROM
UNITED CHURCH PRESS

770606

Copyright © 1976 United Church Press
All Rights Reserved

No part of this publication may be reproduced, stored in a retrieval system, or transmitted in any form, or by any means, electronic, mechanical, photocopying, recording, or otherwise, without the prior permission of the publisher.

Library of Congress Cataloging in Publication Data

Warford, Malcolm L 1942-
The necessary illusion.

"A Pilgrim Press book."
Includes bibliographical references.
1. Christian education—United States. I. Title.
BV1467.W37 1976 268 76-18840
ISBN 0-8298-0311-4

Biblical quotations marked NEB are from *The New English Bible* © The Delegates of the Oxford University Press and the Syndics of the Cambridge University Press, 1961, 1970. Reprinted by permission.

Portions of chapter 5 are taken from the author's article "Education, Theology and Liberation" published in *Lumen Vitae*, XXIX, 1974/1, pp. 97-103 and in *The Living Light*, II, 1 (Spring 1974), pp. 60-77. Used by permission.

United Church Press, 1505 Race Street, Philadelphia, Pennsylvania 19102

TO
HARRY R. WARFORD
M. OWEN KELLISON

But take good care: be on the watch not to forget the things that you have seen with your own eyes, and do not let them pass from your minds as long as you live, but teach them to your sons and to your sons' sons.

—Deuteronomy 4:9, NEB

CONTENTS

PREFACE 9

CHAPTER ONE
THE DUBIOUS PARTNERSHIP 13

CHAPTER TWO
THE REVERENT SPECTATORS 27

CHAPTER THREE
CONNECTIONS 41

CHAPTER FOUR
CONTEXTS 53

CHAPTER FIVE
CONSCIOUSNESS 63

CHAPTER SIX
TOWARD NEW OPTIONS 75

NOTES 89

ABOUT THE AUTHOR 95

PREFACE

> Hardly is the cry of "Fire!" heard before a crowd of people rush to the spot, nice, cordial, sympathetic, helpful people, one has a pitcher, another a basin, the third a squirt . . . so eager to help put out the fire.
>
> But what says the Fire Chief? The Fire Chief . . . he says, or rather bawls, "Oh, go to hell with all your pitchers and squirts."
>
> —Soren Kierkegaard[1]

The most critical educational concern in the churches should be how the local congregation can represent in its life a transforming and liberating community of faith. Too often, though, we have bypassed the difficult issues of purpose and meaning and turned this central concern into an engineering problem which we have tried to solve through gimmicks and techniques. Each year we tend to adopt the latest device invented by popular psychologists, management consultants, or public educators. As these periodic fads come and go, the educational crisis remains.

The more obvious signs of this crisis center in the declining numbers of children enrolled in Sunday schools, the shrinking financial resources for professional educators on both the local and national level, and the continuing conflict over the nature of content and process in religious education. The lure of conservative church growth has pushed some churches toward imitating the yellow bus brigade and the mercantilistic and competitive practices of some fundamentalist Sunday schools. More often than not we have tried to bolster enrollment and seek funding without confronting the hard demographic facts which point to a declining birthrate, especially in the middle-class families who make up most of our congregations, and to marginal growth, if any, in the churches' membership.

In regard to the Sunday school, Robert Lynn has suggested that the erosion of this once-venerable institution in the liberal churches is connected with the disappearance of evangelicalism within mainstream Protestantism. He points out that in those churches where evangelicalism is the predominating style of church life, the Sunday school is a strong and viable educational strategy. But in the liberal Protestant churches where the evangelical emphasis on personal conversion, revivalism, and individualistic morality is absent, the Sunday school is in a weakened state. Implicit within Mr. Lynn's analysis is the assumption that the educational crisis is a sign of the disappearance of white, Anglo-Saxon, Protestant culture as the predominating tradition in American society. The emergence of a pluralistic society has eroded the once-established place of the Protestant churches in the American mainstream.[2]

My hunch is that we have again been guilty of approaching a crucial situation with pitchers and squirts when more critical response is needed. Indeed, our definition of the problem itself constitutes a primary difficulty. As long as we see the educational issue as simply one of updating or modernizing our methods, our solutions will continue to ignore the real problems. For in the words of Paul Tillich, "The problem of the Church School is more than the problem of a particular educational aim. It is the problem of the relation of Christianity and culture generally and Christianity and education especially."[3]

In the following chapters I want to focus on education in the context of the church. The first chapter deals with the traditional patterns of religion and education in American culture and the strategies which were developed by religious educators to meet the perceived needs of this situation. The second chapter, "The Reverent Spectators," explores some impressions of life in the contemporary church in an attempt to articulate the themes of alienation and confusion which beset liberal churches. Chapter Three depicts three myths of transcendence and their impact on our images of the church and its purpose in our lives. Chapter Four picks up the theme of integrity and transformation in order to suggest a tentative definition of Christian education. It emphasizes the context of education in the local parish and the necessity for educators to deal with the environment of learning itself. The next chapter explores the development of critical thinking in the church as an educational task; it outlines some of the work of Paulo Freire as a way of looking at some meanings of transformation. The final chapter, "Toward New Options," extends the discussion of the church's culture and the problem of educational change and tries to deal with some implications of the preceding discussion. Throughout the book my aim is to address the educational crisis in the liberal Protestant churches.

My hope is that the educational mission of the church can center in the continuing task of creating and renewing the church as an instrument of faith. This necessitates our ongoing effort to maintain the community's integrity in the face of all the demands to diminish the significance of its substance and to defer its calling to be a center of human transformation. The revolutionary option available to us begins when we recognize the praxis of action and reflection appropriate to our milieu, rather than stylistically trying on liberation in the manner in which the emperor appropriated his new clothing. The hope that the church can be the body of Christ, a symbol of a transcendent reality, may be illusory in the sense that we can never adequately fulfill the markings of this community of faith; but the vision of a peaceable kingdom, the pull of the purposes of God, and the image of Jesus as the Christ make this the only necessary illusion.

—Malcolm L. Warford

CHAPTER ONE

THE DUBIOUS PARTNERSHIP

> As a baptized child of the church I knew that Jesus was important; and as a reader I knew he made some memorable statements. But I was not as fond of him as I was of Santa Claus, for instance, or Benjamin Franklin, Abraham Lincoln, and our own Teddy Roosevelt.
>
> —Brooks Atkinson[1]

During my first few days as a minister in a small New England village, I was urged to attend the annual Memorial Day service sponsored by the local elementary school and held in the Congregational Church, to which I had been called as pastor. As in many villages, the white spire of the meetinghouse overshadowed all other buildings on the town common. Although the church itself no longer occupied an officially established position in the community and most villagers had little formal relationship with the parish institution, practically everyone considered himself or herself to be "mildly Protestant." The church was there for the ritual occasions of life—birth, marriage, and death. It was used to express these events in symbol and ceremony. In this particular village, if anyone really "got religion," he or she usually ended up in the recently established Bible Baptist Church or became involved with the local group of Mormons.

When everyone had assembled in the church on Memorial Day, the children entered the nave and moved forward to position themselves at the front of the chancel. The scene was set by the placement of an American flag in a stand on top of the communion table. (In the background I detected the presence of an electric fan which encouraged the stars and stripes to unfurl in a dependable and constant breeze.) The program began with a teacher's statement about the significance of Memorial Day. Then some of the children recited poetry with themes of God and country, sacrifice and valor, which they had memorized especially for the occasion. The affair ended with the whole group singing patriotic songs and the children's chorus rendering a special arrangement of the then popular "Ballad of the Green Berets."

Later, as I became acquainted with some of the participants in the Memorial Day service, I discovered that a number of them were members of the church. Some of the teachers taught in the public school and the Sunday school as well. Even the woman who accompanied the school chorus was the church's organist on Sunday morning. In fact, most of the children had sung the Memorial Day songs in the church service on the preceding Sunday as members of the youth choir. For many adults and children alike, however, it did not much matter whether the program was sponsored by the school or the church because as far as they were concerned it was the same in either place. Both the church and the public school were suitable settings for communicating the patriotic and vaguely Christian ideas of right and wrong, "goodness" and the good life, contained in this public's faith.

This situation contains the outlines of the entangling alliance between the Protestant churches and American civil piety. In particular, it points to the typical parallelism which has existed between the public school and the Sunday school. Robert Lynn has suggested what this "parallelism" has signified for Protestants:

> A "blank check" confidence in the public schools, a corresponding optimism about the adequacy of slender marginal efforts in church education (that is, the Sunday school), and a conviction that these parallel institutions, although under different auspices and bound by somewhat different curricular responsibilities, were still yoked by a common concern for moral education.[2]

Before we dismiss the bad taste or theological inappropriateness of the Memorial Day event in the New England village as yet another example of cultural lag, we need to consider it within the context of the "parallelism" which Mr. Lynn describes and to examine the dubious partnership which has existed between Protestants and the American public. In order to be more clear about who we are and where we might be going, it is important that we have some idea of the past which has brought us to our own ambiguous moment.

The story begins, like most American narratives, on a ship coming from Europe, with the Puritans' appropriation of the Old Testament idea of an elect people and a promised land. It begins with a covenant made between a people and God; and another covenant, or more appropriately a social contract, a constitution, agreed to by a later group of colonists in pursuit of the Enlightenment ideals of life, liberty, and happiness. Patriotic piety has its roots in the myths and symbols of the early Puritans and the later founding fathers, who saw America as God's latest experiment and the course of this nation's history as none other than the promise of Providence being worked out in the natural ordering of things. Within this context, the nation itself and not the church as a disciplined body of believers was the locus of God's grace. The sacred history was the nation's history. The churches were there to inspire, comfort, and occasionally chastise, but theirs was an auxiliary rather than a central role.

Indeed, the term "Protestant" came to refer more to an ethos which combined parts of the gospel with patriotic faith in America than to the specific creeds of confessional traditions. The piety and politics of this Protestant ethos were nurtured by the growing influence of revivalism as a personal experience of conversion and a means of social reform. The revivalists took religion out of the churches and into countless tents and meeting grounds. The nation itself cultivated a churchlike soul; and the churches, in order to survive, had to develop a nationalistic spirit. Evangelists and politicians alike took history from the hands of a sovereign God and placed their hope in the work of a converted people and a righteous empire. Piety, then, took on a patriotic commitment and politics nurtured an evangelical tone.

As the population shifted in the early 1800s from the East Coast to the Mississippi Valley, there was deep concern in the East that the valley's inhabitants would revert to barbarism unless "Christian civilization" was taken to them. This concern evolved into a massive educational enterprise composed of revivals, schools, churches, and publications. Protestants initiated, staffed, and financed these various reform endeavors as a way of extending their own ethos and guaranteeing the continuation of the institutions they felt to be important to the future of the Republic.

Haphazard though this Protestant reform effort may have been in its original construction, it was nevertheless effective in helping to construct a definition of American culture which only recently has reached a point of critical challenge and distress. Perhaps most of us raised in this milieu are so close to it that we cannot see it. But the immigrants saw it. Catholics and other aliens in the midst of this Protestant Zion recognized the demands it made on them to cast off their particular ethnic identifications if they were to become Americans. "We welcome the German or the Irishman," Theodore Roosevelt asserted, "who becomes an American. We have no use for the German or the Irishman who remains such."[3] To be an American, therefore, was to be white, preferably Anglo-Saxon, and Protestant, or at least to become as much like this model as possible.

Although the public schools were not formally related to any Protestant institution, they were largely established and supervised as one facet of Protestant reform efforts in the nineteenth century. Along with the churches, the public schools became the primary centers for the nurture of the Protestant ethos and American civil piety. For many persons, the moral education offered by the schools and the ethics cultivated by the churches were identical. God and country, cross and flag, church and school—it made little difference which was emphasized because in the popular mind they were essentially the same.

This amalgamation was demonstrated for me in the middle 1960s when I was teaching elementary school. In 1963 the Supreme Court ruled against Bible readings and prayer in the public school. Soon after the court's ruling, our Superintendent of Schools sent out persons to collect classroom Bibles and distribute manuals on citizenship. Teachers were instructed to take the time usually set aside for morning devotions and use it as a period for citizenship instruction and values education. We were to read a page a day from the manual and to discuss with the children various national heroes and events which inspired patriotism. Needless to say, the transition from Bible to manual was hardly noticed by my students.

Both the public school and the Sunday school have been concerned with fostering the child's faith in that loosely knit collection of affirmations which marked the American Protestant ethos. The piety sustained in the public school during the week was reinforced in the various church schools on Sunday. The two schools enjoyed a symbiotic relationship. In *Guardians of Tradition,* Ruth Elson has outlined the contents of the ethos shared by public and sectarian schools:

1. Nature operates according to the immutable laws of God.
2. History moves toward perfection.
3. Individuals can be characterized by readily available stereotypes of ethnic and cultural groups.
4. Virtue and vice can be appropriately rewarded and avoided by following certain prescribed rules.

In addition, Ms. Elson points out that public school textbooks were permeated with the belief that America was God's hope for the world and democracy his form of government.[4]

Chief among the textbooks used in the schools were William Holmes McGuffey's *Eclectic Readers,* which collected fables, poems, essays, and biblical stories into a series of readings appropriately graded for various ages. The contents of the *Readers,* of course, underscored and reiterated the values of the predominating culture. They filtered civil piety and Protestant virtues through the lens of the middle-class, small-town view of life. Such phrases as "Try, try again," "Where there's a will there's a way," and countless others contained in the McGuffey readings became standard parts of American popular speech.[5]

William McGuffey, like many other textbook editors, was a minister as well as a teacher. He drew no lines between the public schools and the Sunday schools in terms of moral education. Between the schoolbooks and the Sunday school literature there emerged a new communion of secular and sacred saints. Jesus and Abraham Lincoln, Moses and George Washington, were just a few of the persons who appeared in this uniquely American canon.

The difference between the idealized version of American piety and its actual practice in everyday life was often an irresistible source of humor for the novelist Mark Twain. His sensitivities to the moral currents of the nineteenth century give us an exceptional insight into the state of public piety as seen by this acerbic critic. Besides the well-known stories of Tom Sawyer, Huckleberry Finn, and the prototypical Widow Douglas, one short story especially describes the piety of the period.

In "The Story of the Good Little Boy," Twain told of a young boy, Jacob Bliven, whose highest ambition was to get his picture in a Sunday school book.[6] Jacob was aware that in the books good little boys often died, but he was nevertheless still attracted to daydreaming about possible scenes which might be included in such a pious book. One image portrayed his "refusing to lie to his mother, and her weeping for joy about it." Another appealing picture showed him giving a penny to a poor woman and admonishing her not to be extravagant. In order to make his ambition come true, Jacob tried to be as good as possible. He obeyed his parents, did his lessons at school, and was never late for Sunday school. He did not play hookey, refused to rob birds' nests, and "he wouldn't give hot pennies to organ-grinders' monkeys." Jacob's pursuit of goodness was derived from what he read in the Sunday school books. "He believed," Twain wrote, "in the good little boys they put in the Sunday school book; he had every confidence in them." Although Jacob never came across one of these good boys in real life, he nevertheless followed them as models for himself.

The problem which faced Jacob, however, was that things never worked out for him the way they had worked out for all those good little boys in the Sunday school books. His virtue was not rewarded. Whenever he tried to be good in the manner described in the books, he always seemed to get into trouble rather than be rewarded for his good works and intentions. For example, Jacob had read that bad boys who stole apples usually fell from the tree and broke their arms as a just punishment for their misdemeanor. When Jacob came upon a bad boy in the act of taking apples from someone else's tree, he felt obliged to tell the boy what his certain fate (according to the Sunday school text) would be if he pursued his wrong ways. As it turned out, the boy did fall from the tree, just as the text predicted, but he fell on Jacob, who was the one who got the broken arm.

Twain's cryptic representation of middle-class manners and quasi-religious morality suggests the tensions between sincerity and authenticity. His barbs catch on the incongruities between professed morals and actual behavior. His incisive critique of the predominating climate of opinion suggests that the Protestant ethos was more pronounced in rhetoric than in actuality. The heightened emphasis on rural values, the negative graces (not smoking, drinking, dancing, or swearing), and the righteousness of the converted suggest that the situation in the nineteenth century was other than the official consciousness portrayed it to be. Nevertheless, the image is there, and it was a perceptual system which defined the cultural setting in terms acceptable to the Protestant middle class, who were the dominant Americans.

The world of Mark Twain's novels and McGuffey's *Readers* underwent significant change by the turn of the century, as industrialization and modernization began to change rural small-town America. Evangelicalism passed into Progressivism, and the city emerged as the central scene of the nation's development. If McGuffey had been the Confucius of nineteenth-century America, and this was the title given him by the journalist Mark Sullivan,[7] then the Confucius for the twentieth century was to be John Dewey. Unlike McGuffey, however, Dewey was not confident that the traditional agencies of schooling could provide for the public's education in the increasingly technological and urban society. "It is obvious," Dewey wrote in 1899, "that our social life has undergone a thorough and obvious change. If our education is to have any meaning for life, it must pass through an equally complete transformation." The means Dewey chose to accomplish this transformation was the school as an "embryonic community."[8] If the conditions of life had changed to such an extent that a child could no longer be educated informally through contact with community institutions, the school's responsibilities had to increase to make up for this growing lack. The school, then, was to establish an environment for learning which re-created the fabric of society, now torn by the process of industrialization. The school was to become the little community which assumed the traditional responsibilities once carried out by the larger society in an earlier time: namely, the special tasks of induction and initiation into society.

Dewey was aware that the traditional school was not designed for these larger purposes. The nineteenth-century school had shared its responsibilities with the family, the church and its Sunday school, and other community institutions. Dewey himself had grown up in Burlington, Vermont. In this small town he had come in contact with a variety of persons who had introduced him to different skills and experiences. He saw men working at their trades as he walked down the main street. In a few minutes he could go beyond the town limits and see at first hand the production of food and clothing on nearby farms.

Moreover, the town itself was an educational setting in which Dewey not only observed skills but was also brought face to face with attitudes and values which provided the context in which these various experiences occurred. The political process was not remote but very near, for it was carried out by neighbors and townspeople whom Dewey knew and recognized from daily life in the community.

Dewey's own move from small-town Vermont to Chicago and later to New York personally expressed the displacement which was taking place throughout American society. He was concerned about the possibility of democratic education when participation in the events of growing up were further and further isolated from immediate observation and participation by youth. Dewey proposed that the school assume the responsibilities once carried out by parents, church leaders, and other community elders. This meant significant change within the school's pedagogy and program. The child needed physical room and psychological space within which to explore and to experience this world in miniature. The teacher was there to nurture those educational events which in an earlier time would have come naturally to the child by his or her life on the farm or in the village. The school was to become, in Dewey's words, the "child's habitat," where he or she learned through participating in a miniature community, an "embryonic society."[9]

Dewey's educational concerns shared the social reconstruction goals of the progressive movement in politics. The school was self-consciously a means of social progress. More than this, however, Dewey's reform was in a sense a last effort of white, mildly Protestant Anglo-Saxons to establish their culture as the definitive expression of being an American. The school, then, was an agency of acculturation into this particular cultural experience.

It is not surprising that education took on religious connotations for Dewey. Although he had little patience with formal religion, Dewey understood the search for the common good, the building of a free and just society, as an essentially religious endeavor in its concern for the ultimate matters of personal and social life. The school served somewhat the same purpose as the church in communicating and confirming persons into the culture. The teacher in turn was to be the "prophet of the true God and the usherer in of the true kingdom of God."[10]

Edward Ross, a sociologist and a contemporary of Dewey, went so far as to suggest, "The ebb of religion is only half a fact. The other half is the high tide of education. While the priest is leaving the civil service, the schoolmaster is coming in. . . . Step by step with disestablishment of religion proceeds the establishment of education."[11]

Dewey, then, represents the pivotal point at which the school became the unofficial established church of the nation. The school took on new power in Dewey's reform, and this power was increased as the public school system grew throughout the country to be the almost exclusive means of educating children and youth. The energy once invested in trying to create the kingdom of God through individual conversion was transferred to the progressive hope of instituting the great democratic society by free public schooling.

Parallel with the rise of progressivism in politics and education was the emergence of a progressive movement in church education. Educators such as George Albert Coe, William Clayton Bower, and Harrison Elliott were concerned about the task of reconstructing both church and culture through the liberal vision of a free and democratic society. In 1903 the Religious Education Association was organized as a platform for the progressives who, in their own words, wanted "to inspire the educational forces of the nation with the religious ideal and to inspire the religious forces of the nation with the educational ideal."

In advocating a progressive understanding of education, these religious educators encouraged concern for the psychological foundations of education, suggested nurture as a key to the learning process, and tried to reform the traditional Sunday school into a modern agency of change and innovation in line with John Dewey's educational philosophy. Moreover, they attempted to develop a group of professional religious educators in the churches to replace the itinerant volunteers of the past. Finally, they sought to make a place for religion in the public schools both as an academic subject and as a qualitative concern for the values which the schools communicated.

Although these religious educators were very much concerned with change, they were also agents of continuity with past commitments between Protestants and the public order. The unity of Christian purposes and American ideals was an assumed partnership. Furthermore, they shared progressive education's faith in the public school as the primary educational agency in the twentieth century. The public school was their point of reference in trying to transform the Sunday school and the churches' educational programs.

Most religious educators were largely uncritical of the entangling alliances between church and culture. They adopted the norms and procedures of progressive education without examining its cultural origins and presuppositions. They struggled to free the churches and their educational activities from the older evangelical theology, with its emphasis on personal conversion, revivalism, and social conservatism. But they did not attempt to ferret out the other facet of that evangelical enterprise, which was the effort to make religion support democracy. The religious educators simply continued, though transmuted in different tones, the essential and assumed oneness of Protestant Christianity and American culture. Rather than challenging the public school's growing usurpation of moral education, they encouraged the school's efforts and promoted its quasi-established status. Although critical of the churches' educational practices, the religious educators were often uncritical of the public school's pedagogy.

The religious education movement reached its height of influence in the 1920s. The economic crash of 1929, however, brought a halt to many of the innovations evoked by the movement. This financial factor, combined with an emerging theological critique of the movement's liberal theology, limited the direct effect of the religious educators on the church at large. In retrospect, however, one sees that the progressive educators were influential in the modest growth of a group of educational leaders in the theological schools and denominational agencies. Although many parishes could not afford to employ a full-time director of religious education, there did emerge an association if not a profession of such persons throughout the country. One sign of the impact of the progressives was the gradual shift from adult-modeled forms of curriculum toward the creation of graded materials sensitive to child growth and development.

The issues and questions raised by the religious educators remain some of the key concerns of Christian education today. The nature of the Sunday school, the need for alternative forms of church education, the relationship between theology and education, and the complicated issue of religion and public education are still central problems.

It is evident even from this cursory look at religious education in American culture that the churches' educational concern was part of a larger architecture of learning supported and sustained by white, largely Anglo-Saxon, middle-class Protestants who were anxious to mold the morality of the nation along the lines of their own particular ethos. The church was an assumed and established part of this larger cultural pattern. It accepted the culture's support and reduced the lines separating its life as a distinctive faith community from the life of the middle-class community at large.

With their substance defined essentially by the culture in general, churches in modern society have found their purpose in serving community needs. For the educational enterprise in the parish this has meant supporting those parallel organizations in the community which, broadly conceived, are understood to be agents of Christian education. The Boy Scouts, Girl Scouts, YMCA, YWCA, and DeMolay are just a few of the community organizations which have been vested with spiritual as well as civic significance. The public school, however, remains the center of this educational configuration. The parallelism of the nineteenth century which envisioned the public school and the Sunday school to be partners in a common task of moral education continues to exist in some places, but more and more the Sunday school has become simply one of many auxiliary institutions related to the "real" school.

Now that the overtly religious character of the public school has been made illegal by Supreme Court rulings, the quasi-religious quality of public education is less evident than it once was when Christmas pageants and Easter egg rolls were part of the school year. This means that the values communicated in the schools are less connected with Protestant piety. It does not mean, however, that moral instruction is absent. Indeed, the so-called neutrality of the public schools has become a shibboleth which veils much of the ethics and attitudes cultivated in the classrooms and extracurricular activities of the schools. Despite periodic attempts to teach religion as an academic subject or to establish released-time programs for religious instruction, the churches have had little impact on public education. We continually attempt, however, to imitate the public schools and to use their evaluative criteria for judging our own efforts in Christian education.

At times the church has stood in tension with the morality of the majority, yet more often than not we must admit that Jesus has been simply one of several heroes of the American way of life. Our partnership with the public schools has been a dubious one at best. However convenient this vague educational arrangement may have been in an earlier time, it is a futile strategy for our present situation. Only the romantic mind-set could maintain that the village patterns of nineteenth-century America are appropriate guidelines for today.

CHAPTER TWO

THE REVERENT SPECTATORS

> The old Malvern, which is gone forever, is more real to me than the new one that now exists. It molded impulses and instincts that still move me every day. It aroused obsessions that still haunt me. It kindled longings I will feel until I die. Malvern was the place where, as I might once have said, and can still say in another way, "Jesus came into my heart," where the awful sense of the fathomless mystery and utter transiency of life first dawned on me, and where I discovered that in the midst of all that terror and nothingness I was loved. What more could anyone's tribal village do for him?
>
> —Harvey Cox[1]

As Harvey Cox indicates, the Malvern, Pennsylvania, he remembers is no longer present. The patterns of community life have changed and significant persons have died or moved as the 1930s village has become a 1970s suburb. The village is no longer a reality except in its continuing impact on Cox's own life. This Protestant community has faded not only from Harvey Cox's experience but from our own experience as well. As I tried to demonstrate in the preceding chapter, it is the disappearance of the traditional patterns of Protestant community life which lies at the heart of the educational crisis in the church. The dramatic changes which have occurred in our society in general have established a broad context of alienation and distress which cannot help but be reflected in the churches. We live in an era of change, turmoil, and shifting values. We have developed a society filled with the technological wonder of incredible inventions and techniques which have transformed within a relatively short time the face of the earth and the fabric of our culture. Like the sorcerer's apprentice, though, we find it difficult, perhaps even impossible, to restrain the uses of technology against our own best interests. We have been accustomed to presuming the unlimited capacity of the earth to expand in proportion to our growing demands. We have not yet confronted the need for control of exploding populations, the use of natural resources, and the massification of human beings in a collectivized society. The technological crisis is intensified by the continuing threat of nuclear war, world hunger, and cultural unrest.

While we often speak of tragedy in the personal sense as something which happens to individuals, we have all shared the public crises of the last decade in the United States. What does it mean for us to have witnessed the assassination of a President, the murder of his brother, and the slaying of a civil rights leader such as Martin Luther King, Jr.? As a people we have experienced the horror of a meaningless war, the hardship of a continuing economic crisis, and the disillusionment of seeing the sordid self-righteousness of a President guilty of criminal acts. How are we to interpret these events? How can we even pretend to make sense out of them when in truth we know they are senseless? If as individuals we can absorb only so many crises before becoming ill ourselves, is not our culture itself in the throes of an emotional breakdown as well?

Most of us are involved in this cultural crisis at different levels. Just as we are able in times of individual tragedy to reexamine our lives and begin again, or retreat and die to the world, or simply repress what has happened and pretend nothing is changed, so are we able in this period of turmoil to choose one of these three options. As in the facing of death, our tendency is to deny the reality of the situation. Yet something has undeniably happened. Despite our denials, the old confidences are eroding, and though we may pretend that we are not in an era of transition, we need only look at such institutions as family, church, and school to perceive the continuing erosion of traditional authority. Moreover, the frail legitimacy of these national institutions points to the even more fragile appeal of the American dream itself, the traditional cluster of images and ideals which have represented the American way of life. Perhaps no person has expressed this working vision more succinctly than did former President Richard Nixon in his acceptance speech to the Republican convention in 1968.

In one portion of the address, Mr. Nixon linked his own personal dream with the American dream and spoke of himself in the following way:

> I see another child.
>
> He hears the train go by at night and dreams of faraway places he would like to go.
>
> It seems like an impossible dream.
>
> But he is helped on his journey through life.
>
> A father who had to go to work before he finished the sixth grade sacrificed everything so his sons could go to college.
>
> A gentle Quaker mother with a passionate concern for peace quietly wept when he went to war but understood why he had to go.
>
> A great teacher, a remarkable football coach, an inspirational minister encouraged him on his way.
>
> A courageous wife and loyal children stood by him in victory and defeat.
>
> In his chosen profession of politics, first scores, then hundreds, then thousands, and finally millions worked for his success.
>
> Tonight he stands before you—nominated for President of the United States.
>
> You can see why I believe so deeply in the American dream.
>
> For most of us the American Revolution has been won; the American dream has come true.[2]

The irony, of course, is the way in which this very dream became a source of corruption not only for Mr. Nixon but for the nation as a whole. We find ourselves with the rhetoric of freedom, individualism, and conquest at a time when the great needs are compassion, cooperation, and wholeness. Whether we can move toward a broader and more human vision of the world is a crucial issue, especially for a people who have been accustomed to seeing their own ethos as the ultimate reality.

An ethos is something we usually look for in a people foreign to ourselves. We are curious, for example, about how the natives in Samoa come of age, yet we are strangely silent on our own formation. The problem is that what the observer calls an "ethos" is the observed's reality. It is a denuding experience to become self-conscious about our own way of life as an ethos: that is, a pattern of beliefs and behaviors which collectively communicate a spirit of life. In reflecting on his own coming of age in Melrose, Massachusetts, at the turn of the century, Brooks Atkinson, the drama critic, writes, "We had never heard of the 'Protestant Ethic,' and would not have known what it meant if we had heard it mentioned. But now I realize that we were living the 'Protestant Ethic' instinctively."[3] In particular, Mr. Atkinson notes the influence of special institutions and the way some adults gave him a sense of who he was and some hope of what he could become. The public school, the Congregational Church and its Sunday school, the town library, and the community newspaper were just a few of the settings in which Brooks Atkinson instinctively learned the ethos or ethic of the American dream.

Brooks Atkinson points to a more serene, less displaced, time in America. The early 1900s was a world of certainties and eternal verities where life was hard, but it held out promise of success for those who persevered. God was in his heaven and, though all might not be right with the world, there was little doubt that America contained the best the world had to offer:

> It was the best of times. . . . The intangible glories of adulthood promised a bright future. I could imagine myself rising triumphantly to a position that would provide me with a comfortable living—always the principal concern. America seemed to be a dynamic nation full to the brim of possibilities.[4]

The 1900s began with all the confidence that belief in progress could muster. The cultural life of the nation was undergirded by the assurance that history was an evolving process which would get better as society advanced technologically. There was little thought about the threat of development and the negative effects of rapid industrialization.

It is this sense of unlimited possibility which has been challenged in our time. One shift in the modern world is the emerging recognition that progress is neither as certain nor as inevitable as we once imagined it to be. Yet we cling tenaciously to the old Darwinian illusion. Despite recent studies which note the disappearance of crucial natural resources, we continue to seek the silver lining we have been taught to expect within every dark cloud. Rather than changing our styles of living, we put off encounter with the more dismal facts by optimistically relying on future scientific discoveries to lift us out of the almost certain calamities toward which we are heading. Yet however much we may deny reality in our conscious decisions, there exists a pervasive uneasiness throughout our culture. We have glibly referred to this confusion at various levels as an identity crisis.

Much has been written about the nature of this crisis in our society at large, and more certainly will be forthcoming, yet my concern is with the particular nature of this problem in the church. My image of the issue is formed by the picture of a woman my wife and I observed during a trip to Europe. One day as we were walking in the older part of Geneva, we saw an American woman standing on the porch outside the door of the church where Calvin had preached. She was there when we entered the church and she was still standing there when we left. She wore a straw hat and a printed dress and had on white socks with her tennis sneakers. Under one arm she carried Fielding's *Guide to Europe,* and under the other she held on to *I'm OK, You're OK.*

The image of the lady armed with a tour guide to Europe and a popular manual on the psyche standing outside the doors of Christian orthodoxy has remained with me as a poignant sign of our times. Set loose from the traditional moorings of faith, men and women seek out spiritual meaning in touring the world both literally and figuratively and trying out whatever self-help remedies are being pushed by the Book-of-the-Month Club or the religious academies. Beyond belief, we try to find some ways of believing which resonate with our experience and give some focus to our lives. However, like the lady on the porch of Calvin's church we are sometimes immobilized.

In another sense we are like reverent spectators who roam through the church, observing yet never fully committing ourselves to anything except promises that can be broken in quick decisions without entangling alliances. How does a reverent spectator "participate" in church life? This question at first appears to be a contradiction. How can one be a participant and a spectator as well? In actuality there is no problem, however, as numerous individuals participate in the life of the church yet remain spectators to its center of faith. These persons find themselves strangely attracted to the church but are puzzled by their own continuing lack of belief. In a wry and ironic way, though, such persons observe that suspended faith causes no problems in their assuming leadership in the church. The question of believing is hardly ever mentioned, and one discovers how tiresomely "theological" most church members find it when the issue is raised at all. Thus persons who have not participated in parish life for years are invited to take an official role on a church board in the hope that they will become active again. Or men and women who seem somewhat disgruntled with church affairs are urged to teach Sunday school in the expectation that this will make them feel wanted.

One of the more incisive observers of the religious scene is the novelist John Updike, who in several of his stories draws a portrait of the church and its reverent spectators. In his short story "Museums and Women," Updike compares the church with a museum and suggests, "What we seek in museums is the opposite of what we seek in churches—the consoling sense of previous visitation. In museums, rather, we seek the untouched, the never-before discovered; and it is their final unsearchability that leads us to hope and return." Here the church and the museum are counterpointed in ways which the rhetoric of belief would find backwards. "Hope and return," "the never-before discovered," and "final unsearchability" are phrases which the church would have applied to itself as a center of faith and hope rather than to a museum. Instead, what Updike suggests is the familiarity of church life, which often breeds a comfortable but sometimes contemptible piety.[5]

In another short story, entitled "The Deacon," Updike

explores one man's relationship with a local church. Miles, as the churchman is called, is an over-fifty electrical engineer for whom the church functions as a grounding point in his very mobile life. The church for him is a tattered ark, a museum of his own lost sense of time and timelessness. Like many persons who have at one time or another participated actively in the life of the church, Miles's relationship to the parish is inadvertent if not accidental. "He himself wonders why he is there so often," Updike writes, "how he slipped into this ceaseless round of men's suppers, of Christian Education Committee meetings, choir rehearsals, emergency sessions of the Board of Finance where hours churn by in irrelevant argument and prayerful silences that produce nothing."[6]

Miles, who acknowledges that he is not religious, is bored by ceremony, uncomfortable with prayer, and sees "nothing about his body worth resurrecting." He has related to the church ostensibly "to offer his children the Christian option." When his children leave home, he accepts a job offer in another state and decides to sever his ties with the church after the move. Yet the emptiness of his life soon closes around him in the new setting. With no meetings to attend, Miles faces the boredom of his relationship with his wife, who over the years has passed the time by sewing, dozing, and watching television.[7]

Miles eventually succumbs to his uneasy feelings, goes to church swearing, "I'll be damned if I'll join," and ends up in the Men's Club, the Board of Finance, and the Debt Liquidation and Building Maintenance Committee. In the final scene of the story, Miles attends a committee meeting to which no one else comes. As he wanders through the empty building clutching the church keys, Miles observes the sterile trappings:

> The electric clock in the minister's study has been unplugged. Bogus thrift. There are books: concordances, daily helps, through the year verse by verse, great sermons, best sermons, sermon hints, all second hand, no third hand, worse hundredth hand, thousandth hand, a coin rubbed blank. The books are leaning on their sides and half the shelves are empty. Empty. The desk is clear. No business

> conducted on it. He tests the minister's fountain pen and it is dry. Dry as an old snakeskin, dry as a locust husk that still clings to a tree.[8]

But for Miles, who is himself a locust husk clinging to the church as tree, the sterility of the trappings is irrelevant. For him the bark is dry and rough, but the tree is alive enough and he clings to it. The emptiness of the church is a preparation for the emptiness of death. It is a halfway house to his own mortality, but for Miles that is enough:

> It is enough to be at home here. Nothing now exists but himself, this shell, and the storm. . . . The storm seizes the church by its steeple and shakes, but the walls were built with love, and withstand. The others are very late, they will not be coming; Miles is not disappointed, he is serene. He turns out the lights. He locks the door.[9]

Miles as a churchgoer is every person who in an uncritical way has had a vague hunch that there is something within the church which holds out the possibility of wisdom and power and, perhaps, grace. Although these people have never gone beyond their own cynical reflection on the bogus piety which abounds in the church and in which they knowingly participate, they nevertheless acknowledge a latent interest in the church as a tenacious veteran, "an ancient thing that will not quite die." They seek small comfort in the continuities which the ark holds, though they feel no real confidence in their present experience. A bit of guilt, some hope, and a great deal of ritual in the routines of the church's institutional life complete a crazy-quilt pattern of faith.

As in Updike's story, beneath the whirl of activities in many parishes there often lurks a haunting sense of decline and death. Sometimes in unguarded moments persons reveal the fears submerged beneath the activity of the institution. Recently I attended a meeting of the governing board of a suburban church which, like many others, has had to cut back on its budget and face a declining membership. On this particular evening the board was considering a proposal to install an elevator. There had been much discussion in the past two years about the need for the device. The essential reason given for the installation was that many of the older members of the church found it difficult to walk up the stairs to the sanctuary When the point was made that the parish had done without an elevator for the entire time since the church had been built, the retort was usually, "Well, we've done so much for youth, why can't we do something for the elderly now?" The elevator was a sign of the church's membership trend toward a predominantly elderly congregation. If the church was to be composed essentially of the elderly, the argument seemed to run, then we ought to prepare for that future and try to find ways to make it more comfortable.

Under the surface of the argument, however, was another level of feeling which suggested that the church itself was declining. These feelings emerged toward the end of the meeting when suggestions were made from the floor to use some of the money in an endowment fund for existing programs in the church. The board did vote to release some of this money, but the statement was made that this could not become a standard practice. "In twenty-five or thirty years," one person suggested, "we'll need that money in order to survive." This same individual then raised the illustration of a downtown church which at one time had been a major parish in the city and the nation but was now reduced to a handful of people on Sunday morning who were able to maintain the institution only by the interest on its endowment funds. Other persons in the group took this model seriously and understood the future of their own parish in the same way. The future was seen as one of entrophy: a gradual but continuing decline. There did not seem to be any hope of reversing this process. The cycle seemed set and all that was left to do was to await reverently the predestined outcome.

This talk of elevators for the elderly and living off the interest of endowment funds reveals an absence of faith. The disparity between the church in its ideal form as the body of Christ, the community of faith, and its actual life as an institution in society is of course the continuing problematic. Hardened into concrete forms, molded by its cultural environment, the church can speak only a modest word about itself as a sign of God's presence in the world. The mercurial nature of contemporary theology and the faddist pursuit of periodic relevant issues, for example, mark the faltering confidence of the whole religious enterprise. We have asserted the death of God, then disavowed the Christian atheists, only to celebrate God in hope, play, and fantasy before being called back again to confront the mystery of Jesus as the crucified God. "This general uncertainty," as Peter Berger points out in a classic bit of understatement, "has brought religion into a serious crisis of plausibility."[10]

While the traditional religious answers are suspect, relatively little has changed about the basic dilemmas of the human condition itself. The cycle of life continues to confront us with the perplexities of existence, the crises of conscience, and the haunting specter of our own mortality. If anything, the creation of new ethical quandaries through recent discoveries in such fields as medicine and biology only serve to complicate rather than simplify the human condition.

Through all this the church has been the locus of many attempts to "overcome" the crisis. The so-called religious revival of the 1950s and perhaps the return of a significant number of persons to the church in the seventies can be accounted for in part by the attempt to solve public dilemmas by seeking refuge in the private domains of family and personal life represented in the church. Many persons have seen the breakdown of the public community and sought help in the church as a local community where some plausibility for their lives could be found. Here, with people like themselves, they could remove a layer of public image and luxuriate in questions of meaning. Indeed, as one person told me, "I come to church because it is an unreal world. Here I don't have to deal with reality."

The church's success then in many locales depends on the extent to which it sells itself as a retreat for the private domain. This does not mean that some churches are not trying to be "relevant" to social concerns, but it does suggest the tactic that such concerns are dealt with in a way which ensures that they will remain within the confines of conjecture. Poverty, suffering, and the ethics of success are so separated from the realities of the immediate situation that one can take even radical forays into possible solutions without danger of recrimination or personal change.

The church's programmatic concerns seldom connect with the actual lives and public places of the congregation. As I have tried to suggest, this is not accidental. For it is precisely the random nature of church life which allows the church to continue to attract many persons. Surely this is one reason for the chameleonlike nature of the parish and its changing coloration in terms of program and appeal. In a society bent on do-it-yourself identities, the church barters for the trade like any other self-help agency. In fact, a recent critique of the liberal church has asserted that one of its drawbacks has been its poor packaging of religion as an identifiable and marketable commodity for the consuming public. Dean Kelley, in *Why Conservative Churches Are Growing,* suggests that liberal churches "are not victims of changing times but of internal failure—the inability to provide a needed product or service." The reason liberal churches are losing members, then, is that "They have not adequately understood or performed their essential business: the dispensing of religion."[11] The signs, however, point to the fact that some liberal churches are learning their lesson and minding their business. A recent story in the *Wall Street Journal,* for example, described one suburban parish which is trying to assess the needs of its market and to dispense religion in an attractive package.[12] The rather lengthy title of the news item speaks for itself concerning the thrust of the story:

Tending the Flock
Some Protestant Sects
Survive by Stressing
Needs of Congregation
National Programs Cut Back
By Cash-Short Liberals;
"Compassion Fatigue" Cited.

In analyzing the modest yet marked growth of this affluent suburban parish, the reporter interviewed the minister and some members of the church. " 'The only thing that means anything to me is what happens right here,' said a young family man, socializing during the coffee hour after services.'. . . I joined this church because you can get involved here,' he says. 'There are committees by the thousands. The congregation is alive.' " The minister of the church reiterated his parishioner's concern for local affairs and maintained, "It's hard to get up a lot of enthusiasm for broad social issues. . . . People are suffering from a certain amount of compassion fatigue. We can get more going here on a teenage counselling service for drugs and venereal disease than we ever could on the Vietnam war."

The minister went on in the interview to suggest that his ministry centered in attracting more young persons and demonstrating to them that the church does relate to the personal needs of its members. Without saying so directly, he implied that the church's appeal is based on a tacit agreement to let persons define their own needs and to exclude issues they don't see impinging on their lives: namely, those national issues like race, class, and poverty.

This church, and many others like it, reflects the general malaise of our society. The breakdown of familiar cultural patterns has created an ambiguous moment in which the vestiges of a previous time remain, but without significance for our immediate situations. The separation of the worlds of public and private life has increased so that there is seldom any real community which involves the totality of a person's life. Most of our "communities" are private enclaves of the like-minded who agree not to disagree on anything important. The retreat to the private domain is a way of defending ourselves from the onslaught of a depersonalized world. The problem, though, is the inability of this retreat to provide anything more than vague feelings and itinerant solutions. Furthermore, the tentative nature of our involvement in the private sector leads to few sustained relationships and concerns. We move from one association or issue to another with little sense of connection or continuity with a center which encompasses them all. Like Miles in Updike's story, we tend to use the church as an ark which floats on troubled waters. It is a ballast for our fragmented lives and a companion in a lonely world. And, like this fictional deacon, we are somewhat surprised to find an institution which has survived for so long. There is something of the voyeur in us that watches and waits for its demise. Faith in this context is a private affair, impotent really to effect any change in our lives, much less in the world. We come to church, like Miles, "to share the pride of this ancient thing that will not quite die, to have it all to [ourselves]."[13]

CHAPTER THREE

CONNECTIONS

> Meaninglessness in a society or in any individual life implies the collapse of those subtle connections that enable the person or the community to avail itself of the resources of spirit that inhere in the structure of experience as a persisting faith.
>
> —Bernard Meland[1]

The nuances and feelings which I have tried to evoke as descriptions of the church as I often see and experience it suggest the absence of faith as a deepening and renewing dynamic in our lives. The presence of wonder, the anticipation of new possibilities in individuals and society, and an abiding sense of trust in the ultimate significance of life do not often appear as characteristics of churches or church persons. This does not mean, however, that there are not persons and institutions that are struggling with faith and attempting to establish or regain some sense of the grace of God in their lives. But it does suggest a certain absence of vitality and a pervasive sense of hopelessness about the enterprise itself. Bernard Meland puts his finger on the problem when he points to the relationship between our personal confusion and our faltering structures. He maintains that we have lost the institutional connections which are essential if our personal hopes and possibilities are to be communicated and enacted in structures that sustain and organize life. These structures themselves are tied intimately to the myths which give form to our faith and commitments. The lack of connections, then, is not simply the absence of effective institutional procedures; rather it suggests the deeper and more serious failure of our myths to convey a sense of reality which gives form to the feelings and nuances of our inner lives.

In this chapter I want to look at three myths and examine some of the ways in which they evoke institutional commitments and expectations. We will need to test their adequacy as structures of the mind and instruments of faith which shape the ways in which we act on the thoughts and feelings of our lives.

Before going on to this task, let me clarify what I mean by myth. As "the stories of the gods" in its original Greek definition, a myth is a collection of symbols and images which together represent and explain the deepest concerns and ultimate commitments of life. Myths explain the structure of reality and our place in this reality. They provide models for us to imitate. Thus, myths explain the origins of the world, they present an intelligible picture of nature, they provide sanctions for moral and social values, and they give ultimate significance to our individual passage through the cycle of life. The three myths discussed here are the myth of separation and return, the myth of conflict and vindication, and the myth of integrity and transformation.[2]

THE MYTH OF SEPARATION AND RETURN

The myth of the eternal return is one of the oldest paradigms of salvation in the world's religious traditions. The basic theme is the separation of ourselves from our true home and our return to this sacred order from which we were originally conceived. It is an appeal reminiscent of those earliest struggles of life when, nurtured by the care of our parents, particularly our mother, we first experience their removal from us. The feelings of anxiety created by this separation are alleviated by stories which help us cope with the fear of being lost. The primary theme, for example, of *The Wizard of Oz* is Dorothy's frightening separation from Aunt Em and Uncle Henry, her wandering lost in the land of Oz, and her eventual return home to the heartland of a Kansas farmhouse. The myth evokes the sense of our dependence upon the mother, who gives us a feeling of wholeness. Our concern is to return to this figure, to reestablish the dependent relationship, and to receive the hoped-for comfort. Confronted by the ambiguities and terrors of an often hostile world, we have sought in this myth the establishment of a sacred place, a center on this earth which represents our true home. The symbols and rituals of this sacred place articulate our hope; they give us sanctuary and safety from the powers and principalities that threaten to undo us.

While this myth and its variations play a major role in the Eastern religious traditions, it has been an important theme in Christianity as well. It is easier to perceive the outlines of the myth in the more liturgical churches, where the richness of worship represents these primordial images and feelings, than it is to ascertain these elements within the free church traditions. It is only when we penetrate the worship forms in their less apparent liturgical significance that we find fundamental unities between such seeming opposites as the Catholic mass and the Baptist revival. The mass celebrates the eternal sacrifice of Christ. It places emphasis on the role of Mary as the mother of God and as a co-mediator for us. During the central act of consecration, the bread is broken as an enactment of Christ's suffering and our own human condition. The reception of the wafer and its incorporation in our bodies is an act of wholeness and an experience of communion with God. In the midst of this act of worship, the congregation voices the mythic words, "Only say the word and I shall be healed." The sense of dependency is made clear as a condition of salvation and the reception of the host in the Eucharist. Similarly, the revival actualizes the sacred dependency in the appeal for conversion, the acknowledgment of repentance in the act of coming to the altar in response to the evangelist's call. One gives one's "heart to Jesus" and places trust and confidence in the power of the Holy Spirit and the support of the congregation of those who have experienced a similar conversion. Both Catholic and Protestant experiences are summed up in the words of a hymn written by Cardinal Newman, who at various times in his life was both Catholic and Protestant.

Lead, kindly Light, amid the encircling gloom,
Lead thou me on;
The night is dark, and I am far from home;
Lead thou me on!
Keep thou my feet;

I do not ask to see the distant scene:
One step enough for me.[3]

The myth of the eternal return is the story of alienation resolved through acceptance of a dependent relationship with God. It is the ultimate homecoming. In this sense it is not surprising that a Catholic diocese in the United States made an all-out public relations effort during Advent one year to communicate a message to lapsed Catholics and non-Catholics: "Come home for Christmas." The message was broadcast on radio and television, published in the newspapers, and plastered on billboards. The words resonated emotionally with the appeal of this most basic myth, which articulates the suffering of the world and the ambiguity and alienation of our personal lives. "Come Home" is a primal appeal.

The church within this mythology tends to become the most private of worlds. It is a repository for our fears and hopes; it is the primitive tribe. More and more it falls to the church to become the scene of homecoming, with the congregation an extended family and God the eternal parent. There is a latent tendency for this image to encourage our dependency on God as a compensation for what we cannot do or be in life. This tendency increases as our society grows more alienating and dehumanizing. Symptomatic of this development is the emergence of the Jesus cults among the young. During the past several years we have seen the growth of various groups which articulate a Christ-centered piety and a tribalistic allegiance to a local community which may or may not bear the traditional marks of a church. These groups have been characterized by a literalistic interpretation of scripture, a public and persistent witness of their faith through street-corner testimony or itinerant preaching, and an entrenched loyalty and obedience to the authority of their particular group. Many are communal and live separate from the rest of us in out-of-the-way locations; others have purposely situated themselves in the most public places as a way of drawing attention to their beliefs and practices. These groups constitute a broad spectrum of faith and action. Almost all, however, have attracted young people from the middle and upper classes of America. They signify the presence of apocalyptic visions which suggest that the end of this world is coming soon and the second appearance of Jesus on earth is an imminent possibility. The young people who have been converted to Jesus in these groups universally reject the world and values of the affluent middle-class culture into which they were born and against which they rebelled through drugs, crime, or dropping out. The inescapable conclusion, however, is that they have gotten off one trip simply in order to take another one. Perhaps faith in this context is not another drug, but one cannot help thinking it is an opiate and another way of dropping out. In the so-called Jesus movement, has not Jesus become another countercultural hero and the church simply his groupies?

THE MYTH OF CONFLICT AND VINDICATION

Another alternative myth and one which primarily shapes the religious traditions of the West is the myth of conflict and vindication. It depicts the person's achievement of identity through a moral victory. In the history of religions the conflict and vindication myth, particularly as it has been carried by the Jewish, Christian, and Islamic traditions, has displaced the earlier mythologies of the Middle East, which were primarily nature and cyclical religions of the eternal return. History takes on new importance in this myth because time in this scheme is to be fulfilled by actions which reveal the presence of God in human events. History is no longer seen as a repetitious cycle of events which recur in each generation; in this view, history moves toward a final goal. But just as the person in the myth of the eternal return was incomplete without relationship to an "other" which fulfilled him or her, so in the myth of conflict and vindication the individual is dependent on an adversary for his identity. The stranger, the heretic, or the goy becomes the necessary correlative to the mythic hero, who, by his goodness, overcomes these symbolic powers of evil. David and Goliath, Moses and Pharaoh, Jesus and the Devil represent some of the stories of conflict and vindication which fill the Bible. The myth, however, has become even more powerful in its secularized form. Television, comic books, and movies portray this myth in plots which depend on the ancient struggle between good and evil as the ever-present problem. Superman, Tarzan, and Dick Tracy are just a few of the mythic superheroes in the current media. On a more adult level we may go weekly to various sports arenas to see the competitive morality plays of basketball, baseball, and countless other games which reenact the prototypical duel at high noon.

The problem with the myth of conflict and vindication is that one always needs an enemy. To be the liberator we have to find an oppressor. To be righteous we must search out the forces of unrighteousness. It is the continuing revolution of the saints, be they Puritans in New England or liberationists in Latin America. Ultimately it is a matter of true believers: that is, those who know that truth is on their side and must prove it by condemning others whose beliefs are deemed untrue. If "Lead, Kindly Light" in some sense represents the feelings of the myth of the eternal return, then "Onward, Christian Soldiers" becomes the hymn par excellence of the myth of conflict and vindication.

Onward, Christian soliders, Marching as to war,
With the cross of Jesus Going on before;
Christ the royal Master Leads against the foe;
Forward into battle, See his banners go.[4]

This myth has been a primary influence in the development of Protestant forms of Christianity in the United States. The evangelical awakenings of the nineteenth century established a style of popular religion which has encouraged the acceptance of the crusade as the shape of Christian ethics and reform. Both conservatives and liberals have adopted the crusader's model as the formative influence on social action. The marches of the Women's Christian Temperance Union and the marches of the Southern Christian Leadership Conference were both derivatives of the conflict and vindication myth. The crusading morality that confused America's manifest destiny with Vietnam's future met its radical counterpart in the protesters who demonstrated for peace. Norman Mailer's observations on the encounter between the Army and the peace marchers at the Pentagon in 1967 summarize the problem:

> [The] whole crisis of Christianity in America [is] that the military heroes were on one side, and the unnamed saints on the other. Let the bugle blow. The death of America rides in on the smog. America—the land where a new kind of man was born from the idea that God was present in every man not only as compassion but as power, and so the country belonged to the people; for the will of the people—if the locks of their life could be given the art to turn—was then the will of God. Great and dangerous idea! If the locks did not turn, then the will of the people was the will of the Devil. Who by now could know where was what? Liars controlled the locks.[5]

Both the myth of the eternal return and the myth of conflict and vindication are etched deeply into our psyches. Yet how useful are they as patterns of faith in our world? As dominant themes of identity and religion, they suggest withdrawal and conquest as alternative solutions. Both point to fulfillment outside ourselves as the goal of life. I wonder, though, if the myth of the eternal return, regardless of how comforting it may seem to be, can really enable us to live with ourselves. And, on the other hand, I doubt that the myth of conflict and vindication can help us live with others.

THE MYTH OF INTEGRITY AND TRANSFORMATION

Herbert Richardson has maintained that what we need today is "a new transcendence and identity myth as the foundation of the psycho-social order." For Richardson this myth is emerging as the theme of integrity and transformation:

> The kind of transcendence correlated with the myth of integrity and transformation is that of self-transcendence, expanded consciousness, spiritual rebirth, and divinization. In simplest terms, we may say that the "God" of integrity and transformation is not the one in whom we live (separation and return) or the one who limits and is over against us (conflict and vindication), but the one who lives in us. In our integrity we can experience transcendence as our own potentiality to become more, as the demand for self-transformation.[6]

In speaking of completeness and sufficiency as characteristics of the human being, Richardson does not mean that we should become more isolated from one another. For him, acceptance of the person as having the possibilities of wholeness within himself or herself indicates the opportunity of creating a human community which chooses to be formed rather than forced into being because of the need to be completed by someone or something else. The danger of the myth of integrity and transformation, however, lies in its tendency to fall back into one of the two previous myths, the myth of the eternal return or the myth of conflict and vindication.

Richardson himself reveals the possibility of simply making the myth of transformation another variation of the myth of conflict and vindication—the story of the hero. He uses Kubrick's film *2001: A Space Odyssey* to exemplify his understanding of the myth of integrity and transformation. He points to the independence of the space explorer, who is sent on a voyage accompanied only by a copilot, some other scientists who have been temporarily frozen in still life until their arrival at the future destination point, and a capricious computer called Hal. The movie's plot thickens when Hal decides to take over the ship. He proceeds to cut off the machines that maintain the lives of the sleeping passengers and to kill the copilot. The computer almost succeeds in murdering the space pilot as well, but through several feats of daring and courage the hero overcomes the computer and regains control of the ship. The film ends in a surrealistic scene in which the space explorer undergoes a strange metamorphosis, a rebirth into another kind of organism or consciousness. The point of the film, for Richardson, lies in the transformation event, which he sees as a fulfillment achieved without the intervention of some other power or figure than man himself. The evolutionary process with which the film began, then, is completed in the final transformation of man into a higher consciousness.

Richardson speaks of the myth of integrity and transformation as maximizing the possibilities of human life, yet his depiction of the myth focuses on going beyond the human being, pushing us up and out of the world and toward becoming something other than human. The background music of *2001*, however, clarifies the mythic structure of Richardson's own interpretation of integrity and transformation, for the sounds we hear are taken from Richard Strauss's "Also Spake Zarathustra." The relationship between Nietzsche's superman and Kubrick's space explorer is not accidental, and Richardson's choice of *2001: A Space Odyssey* as an example of his understanding of the myth of integrity and transformation reveals his own dependency on the heroic myth of conflict and vindication, albeit within a twenty-first-century mode. The future of the human being lies beyond man himself; transformation occurs in the act of becoming more than human. The key to our integrity and transformation, then, lies outside ourselves, beyond our present time. A Sufi story which is currently circulating in our society underscores Richardson's point of view;

A man saw Nasrudin searching for something on the ground. "What have you lost, Mulla?" he asked.

"My key," said the Mulla.

So the man went down on his knees too, and they both looked for it.

After a time, the other man asked, "Where exactly did you drop it?"

"In my own house."

"Then why are you looking here?"

"There is more light here than inside my own house."[7]

As told on the lecture circuit or from the pulpit, the story is supposed to inspire us to venture outside ourselves in order to find meaning and significant action. The problem, of course, is that regardless of how much more visibility there may be in the light, the key remains in the darkness and in our situation. In order to find the key and, perhaps, to discover ourselves as well, we need to consider where we are and to perceive this place and time as the context for integrity and transformation.

Integrity and transformation converge in the motif of liberation. The term is currently in vogue with those who are concerned with the inner transformation of our psyches and with others who are trying to effect change in the political and social order. Esoteric philosophies and psychologies of the East, interest in various forms of meditation, and increased scientific research into the nature of the affective and intuitional domains of our brains suggest some of the options now being explored as we try to discern the resources available to us for re-creation and transformation. On the other hand, we have seen the rise of various movements for social and political liberation among the poor, the oppressed, and the disenfranchised. Black persons, Indians, women, and the poor of all races are only a few of the groups which constitute the core of an emerging theology of liberation which articulates the Exodus theme as an interpretation of the rising self-consciousness and protest of the oppressed against the established structures of injustice in the world. It is not my purpose here to describe either the search for inner liberation, nor the quest for social justice and freedom. But I want to point to these two phenomena as signs of the present concern with integrity and transformation. Both movements suggest tentatively an emerging awareness of the unity of the person and the interlocking relationship between social and individual reality, psychological and political liberation. If integrity in some sense is being true to oneself, then transformation is the way in which we achieve this authenticity in our lives. Ultimately it is the movement from death to life, from attachment to the deadly illusions of our society toward a faithfulness which is acted out in the concreteness of response to persons and structures.

Integrity and transformation, for me, point toward the Incarnation, to the image of Jesus as the Christ, the one who lived with integrity and revealed the process of transformation in his life, death, and resurrection. In this context, Jesus is not the one who came from heaven to earth in order to take us back home with him (separation and return); he is not the one who suffered on the cross to pay the gods for our redemption and to lead us in a moral crusade (conflict and vindication); rather, he is the one who shows us what it means to be human. He is the person in the world as life is intended to be and to become. The cross is the point at which Jesus is faithful even in death. Resurrection, then, is the power of that life with integrity and its presence as a transforming image in our present time.

Through the years the gospel has been cast in various cultural models. We have incorporated diverse myths to convey the story of Jesus and to communicate the nature of the Holy. Somehow God has survived all of our various idolatries. The various pseudonyms under which his name has been carried from generation to generation have come and gone as their particular significances in history have vanished. This cannot be otherwise. Each generation must reshape the images of the past in light of its present encounter with the God who meets us in hope as well as memory. The church must be aware of its tradition of faith and concerned about the continuing appropriation and enactment of this faith in its form and mission. For education in the church, this means creating what Bernard Meland termed "those subtle connections" that put persons and groups in touch with tradition and establish the context in which the events of memory are experienced as a contemporary reality. If the processes of education cannot function within the church, this suggests that the most basic values and beliefs of the institution have been undermined. It means that the nature of the church as a transforming and liberating community has been rendered impotent. It acknowledges that the church is not able to confront itself, to look at the great gap between its pretensions and its actuality, and to accept the judgment which must surely come if renewal is to happen. It means that the church has no access to the potentialities of power and presence which are its only safeguard against the cunning manipulations of a world where lives are defined by what they can accumulate, buy, and sell. It means the church has lost its integrity—its faithfulness to that which is holy—and that it has no power to transform and to be in itself a symbol of the transcendent center toward which its language points.

Perhaps the fact is that we have no ethos, no tradition, left in the church except the clichés of American popular culture. Our partnership with American culture, this nation with the soul of a church, may have cost us our own souls. Moreover, what we have interpreted as an established place in American culture has turned out to be simply that unmortgaged space which no one really wanted anyway. In the pursuit of an elusive mainstream location, we have suggested that joining the church is like becoming part of any other well-intentioned group, except that our requirements for membership have been lower. We have prided ourselves on being liberal about believing and behaving when in fact we have simply underscored the lack of any significant articles of faith which do matter. In a situation where we have intimated that it does not make any difference what one believes, we have communicated the fact that "a difference which does not make a difference is not a difference."

CHAPTER FOUR

CONTEXTS

My thesis is that faith is communicated by a community of believers and that the meaning of faith is developed by its members out of their history, by their interaction with each other, and in relation to the events that take place in their lives.

The congregation, then, is a school of faith. All that the congregation does is both a means of communicating the faith and a subject of investigation.

—C. Ellis Nelson[1]

The demise of the traditional parallelism between the Protestant churches and the public sector leaves us facing a gaping hole in our own faith communities. As long as the Protestant version of Christianity was the presumed frame of reference for our national values and mores, there was a vague piety which suffused the whole culture and supported the churches in a quasi-established way. But we now live in a post-Christendom society where the vestiges of this past are few and far between.

We have separated ourselves from the narrow extravagances of evangelicalism only to see ourselves devoid of a living tradition of faith and a viable community of belief. Kierkegaard's lonely polemic against the Danish church suggests language which weights this feeling:

> I believe it is an overstatement to say that Christianity in our time has been completely abolished. No, Christianity is still present and in its truth, but as a teaching, as doctrine. What has been abolished and forgotten, however (and this can be said without exaggeration), is existing as a Christian, what it means to be Christian.[2]

When our peripheral concerns (such as being modern or progressive—or conservative and traditional, for that matter) displace the center which is Jesus as the Christ, the liberator, then there is no nurturing matrix, no substantive tradition which acts as a point of unity and a critical perspective. We become vulnerable to whatever dominates our cultural situation. "We liberals," John Cobb writes, "have come the road from historic Christianity progressively using up the capital of our heritage and doing little to replenish it." And, he continues, "We have come more and more to mirror our culture or certain strands within it, rather than to speak to it an effective word of judgment or healing."[3]

The loss of a conscious ideal is central to the lack of authority in Christian education. No amount of instruction, new curriculum, or teacher training can overcome the absence of a center in the church's life. The problem of education in the church lies in the fact that education cannot do without authority or tradition, yet in the present situation it is difficult to locate either.

The problem, of course, is amplified by the fact that we have lived off the inheritance of halfway covenants for so long that it is questionable whether education as transformation can occur within the existing life of the churches. Ellis Nelson has suggested that faith begins in the community of believers, and John Westerhoff has maintained that religious education is essentially socialization in the church as a subculture, yet the problem for me is whether there is an adult community of faith which is capable of communicating by the form and mission of its life the meaning of the Christian faith.[4] Christian educators have taken the existence of the Christian community for granted. This is our failure. Our hope begins in awareness of this fact.

Let me suggest that Christian education is the continuing praxis of evoking the church's growth as a liberating community and encouraging the development of its critical consciousness. It is the deliberate and sustained effort to communicate the gospel so that persons can accept or reject it. The key word in this definition is praxis, which I would define as action and reflection aimed at transforming the world. Praxis is often understood simplistically as the practical side of any theory, as if a theory does not presume a mode of acting and action does not convey a presupposed theoretical base. The division of theory and practice accounts for much of the abstract nature of theology and the uncritical quality of education. Instead of this arbitrary division, I assume that education includes both theory and practice. Praxis underscores the crucial importance of reflection and critical thinking as inherent parts of the educational enterprise.

Education is centered in change. In the Christian community this means transformation in the image of Jesus as the Christ. The initial concern of church education, therefore, should be the nature of the faith community itself. The regularities of institutional life establish an environment which is the most determinative factor in the actual teaching and learning process. To what extent, it must be asked, is the present church a liberating community which points to and celebrates in its own life the presence of Christ as liberator? In this sense, the educator is concerned with the paideia of the community: that is, the interrelated network of attitudes and values, polity and piety, which forms the context in which learning occurs and from which the church determines its life and mission.

Paideia is a difficult term to define because it is a composite word that refers to a configuration of learning rather than to a specific element of knowledge. Paideia is the accumulative tradition of a community and the processes by which this tradition is passed on; it is the piety, politics, and culture of a people which form the public definition of the person and the conscious ideal of the society. The term points to the deliberate cultivation of a perspective and a way of living derived from the most important values of the community. Paideia, then, is that configuration of ideas and institutions which provides the setting in which a person learns a community's ways of acting, thinking, and feeling. Education, in the sense of paideia, is at the heart of a community's life, and to speak of education in this way is to raise at the same time the predominating commitments and values of the community itself. At this deeper level, education is education for survival. It is the means by which a community sustains its culture and maintains its possible futures.[5]

The milieu, then, not the method, is the ultimate message: that is, the search for methodology in education, while critical, is in itself impotent to effect change. Unless the setting of education is the focus of our concern, and method evolves from this situation, we inevitably engage in generalities and abstractions. Thus it might be helpful for us to think more in terms of paideia than pedagogy and to remember that the latter is derived from the former. Since the social scientists inform us that human beings are polyphasic—that is, we learn more than one thing at a time—is it not important for us to consider the context as well as the content of education? We need to become sensitive to the environments in which we live and to perceive them as conditioning agents which are not neutral but are charged with values and attitudes. The cultural setting, then, is a primary arbiter of our education. It acts for us or against us, but it does not leave us alone. It is critical that we inquire into the nature of the purposes and priorities communicated by the existing regularities of the church's life which establish an environment for learning.

As the church reflects the culture of the society in which it exists, so does education in the church mirror the culture of the parish itself. Therefore, to speak of educational change is to engage in addressing and transforming the situation as well as the formal processes of teaching and learning. Anyone who has served on a church education committee quickly learns that efforts to make significant changes in the educational programs of the parish usually push one toward other aspects of congregational life. For example, I once asked several education committees in various churches to develop a list of the problems they had encountered. The following list is a compilation of the items which appeared continually in the various churches:

1. Too little money.
2. Traditional expectation that Christian education happens only on Sunday morning.

3. Difficulty of communicating the role of Christian education and the problem of being assigned responsibilities which have little to do with education.
4. Lack of parental support in the Sunday school.
5. Difficulty of being able to carry out decisions because of complex and unresponsive church structures of organization.
6. Lack of interest by ministers in education.
7. Competition of worship and education.

This list of problems is a familiar one to persons who have worked with education in the local church. When put together as a configuration, the various items point to the connection between religious education and its institutional context. Let us turn to the Sunday school as a case in point.

Recent debates in church education have tended to focus on the significance of the Sunday school as a means of nurture and instruction. Some argue for the continuation of the traditional model, while others have attempted to modernize the Sunday school by implementing the latest educational techniques. Some critics have suggested the abandonment of the school model entirely, advocating instead a shift to family educational programs, more open learning events, and the adoption of socialization methods as the process of religious education. While this continuing discussion has brought about the development of some significant changes in church education, the focus on the Sunday school and its alternatives in terms of methodology has deflected the debate away from the more systemic roots of the educational crisis. It has established the problem in terms of pedagogy when the real crisis is paideia.

The Sunday school is not only a particular educational method, it is also a visible sign of a more fundamental perception of the church itself. Those who attempt to move beyond the school model must take into account the relationship of this educational strategy to the larger organizational structures of the parish. The Sunday school is no accidental regularity of church life. It points toward a church model which has tended to organize the parish along the lines of secular corporate institutions. This corporate model not only determines the shape of the institution but encourages the growth of self-understandings in the church which are entrepreneurial, market oriented, and efficiency based. Within this model, religion becomes a commodity which is bought, sold, and packaged according to the tastes of its consumers. While we may get rid of the Sunday school and replace it with some alternative model, this does not necessarily indicate that we are making any real change at all. It may simply represent an updating and modernizing attempt to improve the method of communicating a message which remains essentially unchanged. For years religious education has followed the lead of general education in establishing the changing norms for teaching and learning in the church. McGuffey's classroom was replicated in countless church basements partitioned into neat cubicles for Sunday scholars imitating the work of the "real" school. Then we celebrated the age of the child only to find ourselves caught by the same bureaucratic cult of efficiency that smothered John Dewey's progressive vision. We will be no better off in the present day if we go chasing after the latest learning technique now being devised for the public educational system. This does not mean, however, that the Sunday school should not be replaced. It does indicate that before we dismantle this system we need to deal with the church situation in which the educational crisis is located.

In order to perceive the existing paideia in the church, we have to investigate the procedures of governance which control the church in its local reality. This involves an attempt to locate the images which persons hold of the church and which in turn shape the ways in which they approach the politics of parish life. In terms of process, this concern with the institutional setting suggests the continuing attempt to inquire into the relationship between our believing and our doing. It means bringing the gospel to bear on everyday decisions in the life of the church. Unless the faith tradition enters into the deliberations of the church itself concerning its own life, how can we possibly imagine that we can transpose the gospel as a criterion for our own individual lives in society?

While the feeling conveyed by church members is embarrassment over the amount of time spent in committee meetings concerned with the church's business affairs, it is naïve to assume that these meetings are accidental regularities. Indeed, for many persons, such as Updike's fictional deacon, involvement in church life is synonymous with participation in these endless committee meetings. Moreover, there seems to be a growing tendency for parish life to be structured around a calendar created by the annual financial campaign rather than the liturgical year. I have seen several churches where the raising of the annual budget is an all-consuming, year-round affair which dominates the entire program of the church. While the financial drive supposedly occurs only during one of the fall months, the various announcements of budget revisions, final pledge campaigns, and predictions of dire fiscal problems seem to go on continually throughout the year. The effect of this predominating financial drive is the paralysis of church programs, which are never quite sure whether they will be funded, and the more general impression that the church itself is simply a branch of the United Fund.

This concentration of church life into the business of the institution reveals the extent to which the church is understood essentially within a corporate definition. However, the corporate body ultimately acknowledged is not the church as Christ's body in the world; instead, the church is understood as another corporation sanctioned by the state and defined in financial and legal terms. It is not only the visible structures of church organization which reflect this image—that is, the array of boards and committees copied from business management—for it is also the actual legal control of the church vested in trustees which signifies where the power resides. When it comes down to issues that ultimately matter in the life of the church, the last word usually belongs to the trustees, because most crucial issues relate to the use of finances and property. The charade of church life suggests that church authority is placed in the deacons or elders who are responsible for the spiritual affairs of the congregation, but at base the primary issues almost always return to the real elders: namely, the trustees who maintain the state seal of incorporation. The body of state law, rather than the body of Christ, ultimately is the source of power.

For example, in one parish a restructuring committee sought to establish an organizational pattern which was different from the typical one consisting of various boards for each separate function of church life. Instead of this pattern the committee suggested, as a model, one council which would be composed of a group of persons elected as the deacons of the church. These persons then would organize themselves into working groups for the various areas of church life, but the emphasis would be on the unified work of the church and the conjunction of spiritual and financial, program and property, issues in the congregation. On paper this model looked very promising. It seemed to go beyond the usual corporate model of boards to suggest a more theological understanding of the church's system of governance. The promise of this model was violated, however, by one provision which the committee made and the church later adopted: that three of the deacons be named trustees of the church to satisfy the corporation laws of the state. When it was suggested that all the deacons be named trustees, just as all had been named deacons, the motion was turned down because it was felt that only a few persons were competent to hold such a position, though no such objection was raised in the election of all members of the proposed council as deacons. As it turned out, the three deacons who were also named trustees constituted themselves in effect as a separate body from the rest. They maintained final control on all financial and property issues and destroyed whatever promise of a revitalized structure that was present in the proposed model.

This attempt at restructuring church governance illustrates the difficulty of changing the culture of the church. Nevertheless, it is precisely within the existing regularities of institutional life that one needs to move in order to raise consciousness and to work toward systemic changes which alter the paideia of the community. We need to look around to see where the key centers of power are located in the church's structure and to isolate the dehumanizing and liberating themes which are present within its actions and images. We must initiate projects within the church which aim at modifying the way decisions are made, priorities established, and programs supported. This perspective is in direct contradiction to those educational reformers who see a particular educational method as a means to church reform. Improved educational techniques and more humane classrooms will not change the larger patterns of teaching and learning which occur within the structures of the congregation itself. Our task would be infinitely easier if Christianity were simply a body of beliefs to be communicated. Our concern in that case would be that of transmitting a catechism which could be memorized. But the Christian faith is not primarily a belief system, it is a praxis of acting and reflecting within a hope of the reconciliation of man and God. It is a vision of a possible kingdom of peace and wholeness. This hope and vision cannot be taught; it must be communicated in word and deed as well. The ethos of the church therefore must be constantly re-created in each generation and in each local congregation. Its ethic must be enacted in response to the needs of the world in which it finds itself. The continuing temptation is for the church to settle down and work out an arrangement with the surrounding culture which is mutually beneficial. Or else we are invited to close our eyes, shut our doors, and confine ourselves to the church as a remote subculture frozen in the customs of another period and place. In either of these situations, education becomes merely socialization in idolatry, a means of accommodation to the status quo. Christian education emerges only within the context of a liberating community of people who are called to a permanent renewal of structures, individuals who demonstrate in their own lives the possibility of becoming Christian.

CHAPTER FIVE

CONSCIOUSNESS

> I believe that every human being is potentially capable, within his "limits," of fully "realizing" his potentialities; that this, his being cheated and choked of it, is infinitely the ghastliest, commonest, and most inclusive of all the crimes which the human world can assure itself; and that the discovery and use of "consciousness," which has always been and is our deadliest enemy and deceiver, is also the source and pride of all hope and cure, and the only one.
>
> —James Agee[1]

In order for the church to become a liberating community, we need to develop a critical consciousness; we should be concerned with how we can become aware of ourselves and the ideologies that have shaped us. In this sense, transformation occurs in the act of rethinking our everyday worlds of reality. Eugen Rosenstock-Huessy has suggested that conversion or transformation is not so much an act of will as it is "the unwillingness to continue." "This unwillingness," he has maintained, "is not an act but an experience."[2] It is an experience of saying "no" to the way things are in our lives and a rejection of the standards which have been imposed on us and which we in turn have accepted and internalized. It offers the possibility of another way of looking at ourselves and the world. Conversion, within this definition, holds out the possibility of our saying "yes" to an alternative reality.

Education for transformation, then, begins in the critical consciousness of the world views which shape our lives. We need to look at the ideologies which influence our thinking and to break with the myths which determine the significance of our lives. Our immediate task should be to examine critically the symbols and myths which have formed us. This critical task precedes any attempt to communicate the gospel as an alternative view of life. If this critical dimension is absent, all our words of teaching and preaching are taken up and processed by a perceptual system that filters and recomposes the message through a preprogrammed track. The gospel becomes one more component in the Muzak of popular culture.

PAULO FREIRE

One significant help in understanding the development of critical thinking is the work of the Brazilian educator Paulo Freire, who urges us to consider the relationship between education and culture and to expose the naïve assumption that education is neutral toward political and class interests. This perception, of course, is not unique to Freire, yet his own witness to the truth in his life contributes passion and power to his words. Freire has called himself a "vagabond of the obvious," and it was his articulation of the obvious connections between power and oppression which forced him into exile and distanced him from his homeland. Freire was born in the northeast region of Brazil in the city of Recife, where he grew up and worked as an educator until he was forced to leave his country by the military junta which seized control in 1964. Freire was persona non grata because of the revolutionary implications of the adult education projects he had developed in working with the poor of the country. After working in other parts of Latin America for several years, Freire came to the United States in 1969 to join Harvard University's Center for the Study of Development and Social Change. The following year the Brazilian educator accepted a position as secretary for general education in the Office of Education of the World Council of Churches in Geneva.[3]

Paulo Freire begins with the assumption that all men and women are potentially able to act, reflect, and become aware of the social construction of reality. He believes that human beings can perceive the ordered nature of society, take apart the various pieces of everyday reality, and reorder these segments of our experience so that we can understand both the limits and possibilities of freedom in our lives. The problem, however, is that few people believe in their ability to become more fully human. Many persons exist within a mentality which assumes that the nature of reality is ordered and structured by fate in a predetermined and closed universe. Culture is viewed one-dimensionally as a given fact of life which has been created in the past and is the sole arbiter of the present moment. "The way things are," according to this world view, is "the way they have to be," for there is no understanding of the subjective nature of reality.

Freire points to the fact that most of the time our lives are so taken for granted that we seldom pause to wonder about the origin of the thoughts and feelings upon which we act. Much of our behavior is so automatic that we do not often have moments in which we are self-conscious, except, perhaps, in those times when we are embarrassed and find ourselves out of place in a situation. Indeed, we tend to flee from recognizing the conflicting and contradictory elements in life because we uneasily anticipate the upheaval which can occur when the common-sense world is threatened. It is easier to live with the pain of "the way things are" than to experience the conflict of a critical consciousness.

Conscientization, the means Freire suggests to change this condition, is a praxis of action and reflection through which we can discern the social and deliberate construction of reality, identify its oppressive elements, and begin to believe in ourselves as creators as well as inheritors of culture. Conscientization is the task of demythologizing the crippling belief in "the way things are" and trying to re-create the world in ways which dignify our lives as participants rather than as passive observers of life. Freire's literacy method aims at connecting the ability to read with the discovery that the world is made and not simply fated. The beginning point for this literacy method and for the raising of consciousness in general is what Freire terms the archaeology of consciousness. Just as civilizations are layered on top of each other in the same space, Freire feels that consciousness is a complex and layered reality in our lives. As an archaeologist digs, discovers artifacts, rearranges and codes them into meaningful patterns, and is thus able to gain an idea of the culture whose effects he has found, so can the educator problematize the relationship between persons and the world by finding the themes which are present in a given situation, examining the contradicting elements, and together with others perceiving how this culture has come to exist as everyday reality. Like an archaeologist, the person begins with himself or herself as a social product and then self-critically attempts with the help of others to uncover the various levels of his or her life which to this point have been submerged within an uncritical awareness.

When Freire worked with illiterate persons in Latin America, he began by trying to discover the actual situation of the people by observing village life and listening to the villagers' own descriptions of their lives. He would next try to isolate the generative and emotion-filled words which suggested the way in which people perceived their lives. Then, through the use of sketches, photographs, or other visual aids, Freire tried to evoke from these people comments on the nature of their culture. Indeed, the task was to help them realize that they did live within a culture and that they did have a perception of reality. The next step in the process included raising questions about their perceptions and needs and going more deeply into the various levels of contradictions and possible meanings.

A person who participated in Freire's work in Latin America described the process in the following way:

> Freire would go to a village and enter into a conversation with people. He would ask them to help him to observe the village life. He would have them help him take pictures of scenes of village activities which were familiar and common to most of the villagers. The villagers would then come together to see the pictures. Freire would ask them to describe what they saw in detail, writing words under the pictures as they reflected on what they were seeing and feeling.
>
> Then Freire would question the villagers about the contradictions in the explanations which they were giving about why things were the way they were. For example, in one

village, the people described the harvest as being poor. Freire asked them, "Why?" Some of the villagers said, "Because the land is tired." Freire then asked them why some of the land seemed to be very productive and other parts of the land seemed tired. They explained that the rich farmers had fertilizer and they didn't. Freire then asked them how that was the case. The questions and answers continued leading to issues related to their life situation. The topics discussed ranged from those which were primarily theological, political, or economic in nature to those which were basically philosophical in nature.

Frequently, villagers gave fatalistic answers. Freire would always come back to the contradictions which the people themselves had expressed. The people then began, as a result of this process, to think for themselves and to become aware of alternative ways of viewing and coping with what had seemed to be insurmountable problems for themselves and their communities.

In the process, people learned to read, to care, and to have a sense of worth. Freire called what happened to them "*conscientização*" (conscientization).[4]

The heart of Freire's pedagogy lies in his conception of praxis. The coding and recoding of the visual images and patterns of culture becomes a means of increasing critical consciousness of the ways we have been conditioned to think, act, and feel. Through the problematization of predicaments and situations in the life of the community, we can begin to grasp the extent of our manipulation by the dominating forces in society and by our own mute accord with these structures of reality. The growth of knowledge about the archaeology of our consciousnesses emphasizes our right to interpret ourselves and to create rather than simply receive codes of behavior from the established orders of society.

I have discussed Freire's pedagogy of the oppressed as a way of dealing with the process of transformation which is implied by the experience of conversion. The difficulty with this procedure is that we may assume that we can translate this pedagogy directly into the affluent milieu of our society. Paulo Freire confronts the problem directly when he warns of two dangers which plague First World people when we naïvely adopt the pedagogy of the oppressed: the danger of mythologizing the praxis of conscientization and the danger of reducing pedagogy to the level of technique.[5]

MYTHOLOGIZING CONSCIENTIZATION

The mythologizing of conscientization essentially refers to idealization of the praxis so that conscientization becomes a subjective idealism. Rather than being grounded in the actual life of a group, it is disconnected from history and becomes so abstract as idea and process that it has almost no connection with life as it is being lived.

The problem of idealization is most acute in affluent communities, where it is possible to be liberal on social issues without seriously recognizing complicity with the oppressor, for to do so would threaten the affluent life-style to a devastating degree. It is not at all uncommon for various liberation movements in our country to get financial support from the affluent. There is a certain amount of radical chic at work in this phenomenon, but there is also an idealism present which presses individuals to act beyond the comforts of affluence. The difficulty, of course, is that one can be involved with the great issues of war, poverty, and injustice without confronting the connecting questions of "Why am I where I am?", "How did I get here?", and "Do the answers to these questions contribute solutions to the larger issues?" The problem is our facile identification with the oppressed rather than with the oppressor. We identify with the black militants, the farm workers, and the poor. We may even join the movements, but without making any really significant moves ourselves which legitimate this action.

It is in this latter sense that many social activists become part of the problem rather than the solution. The erstwhile efforts of persons who put in their apportioned period of service to the poor before going back to school or returning to their secure status suggest a mockery of the tragic and dehumanizing situations of those who cannot change their lives so easily. For example, many members of Volunteers in Service to America (VISTA) in the southern Appalachian region have raised the ire of the people by their presumptions and uncritical judgments. One woman of the Appalachian region articulated her feelings toward the VISTA workers in the following way:

> I really have this thing with these VISTAs, them coming in here with this idea that we're a bunch of poor ignorant hillbillies. I'm proud to be a hillbilly. And if you don't like the way I talk, then, damn it, go home.
>
> I wonder if these VISTAs ever put the shoe on the other foot and figured if it wasn't for us "poor old ignorant hillbillies" they wouldn't have a damn place to go for them to feel good. But they're gonna make theirselves feel really big. They've all come from upper middle-class families, all had Mama and Daddy handing them everything they ever wanted, ever needed. And as for their college education, take your college educations and shove it.
>
> Okay. That's great. They come down here and they gonna tell me about poverty? They tell us they're frustrated, they can't communicate with these people here. How the hell they gonna communicate with us? They haven't lived our lives. They don't know what it's about. They want to have "gut feelings." All right then, damn it. Give up Mama and Daddy, don't go back in a year. Come down here and spend the rest of your life.[6]

On one occasion I was with the dean of a suburban high school when a young man came into the office dressed in tattered jeans, a faded shirt, and shoes held together with adhesive tape. The young man presented a picture of poverty. The dean casually asked the student why he was dressed in such a style. The student replied that he was just beginning to find out about the roots of his father's life as a young boy growing up on New York's Lower East Side. His manner of dress, he suggested, was one way he could identify with that heritage. Somewhat impressed at least by the sincerity of the student's response, the dean dismissed him without any further comment. A few minutes later I observed the student striding into the student parking lot and driving off in a new MG.

In some ways the boy's feelings of being oppressed were real in the sense of his being confined by affluent structures of his life which made it impossible for him to experience what he had idealized about the authenticity of his father's past. Probably, and I think this is a reasonable conjecture, the student saw himself as politically left of center, maybe even "revolutionary," and striving to be "authentic." Here in effect was Consciousness III, not conscientization.

As you may remember from that distant past of 1970 when *The Greening of America* was first published, Charles Reich's basic argument was that a new consciousness was emerging from the two previous major consciousnesses which shaped American life. Consciousness I centered in the rugged individualism of pre-Industrial America. Consciousness II was related to the technological society and the rise of professional mandarins who trusted reason, expertise, and liberalism. Consciousness III was nothing less than the emergence of a consciousness which was to appropriate the Jewish-Christian ethic. It was "the creative, imaginative, life-giving power of transcendence" which Reich saw transforming American society so that

> the new way of life makes both possible and necessary a culture that is nonartificial and nonalienated, a form of community in which love, respect, and a mutual search for wisdom replace the competition and separation of the past, and a liberation of each individual in which he is enabled to grow toward the highest possibilities of the human spirit.[7]

Reich expected this new way of life to be created by the raised consciousness of young people who were being converted to the new transcendence. The new consciousness would achieve its revolution, he maintained, not through political means but "by changing culture and the quality of individual lives, which in turn change politics and, ultimately, structure."[8]

Although numerous critiques could be made of Reich's analysis, one of the most significant points of debate is his working assumption that "consciousness is prior to structure." According to Reich, the organization of life, the forms of society, follow from the formation of an idealism which evokes the right structures into being. In opposition to this process, Freire would insist that the praxis of consciousness-changing is an interdependent process in which action and reflection are mutual. Without some ongoing action aimed at changing the social reality in which a person lives, there can be no significant change of mind. Conversely, there can be no decisive change in structures if persons simply inhabit new structures with the same old mentalities. The French proverb remains true whenever we choose to separate the two realities: "The more things change, the more they remain the same."

METHODIZING CONSCIENTIZATION

A second danger of an uncritical use of conscientization is to reduce it to the level of method or technique. As Freire suggests, conscientization is not a means of working out problems so that enemies can "love each other as brothers" and "differences be resolved over a good whiskey."[9] Adapting the pedagogy of the oppressed for use in a classroom involves the risk of its becoming "another new thing." No matter how potentially radical a given pedagogy might be for us, this radicality is absorbed within the existing cultural situation if there is not a deliberate concern for change in the social structure itself. The praxis of action and reflection is between ourselves and the controlling order of reality. Whatever the generative themes of freedom and authenticity which are raised in a group, they are ultimately valueless if they are not connected with the larger organization of the given society. Conscientization simply becomes an artifact of progressive education, an instrument of modernization, when it is depicted as a means of "learning by doing."

Another factor in determining whether conscientization is reduced to a small group technique is the absence or presence of risk. One could make the equation: The extent of conscientization equals the proportionate risk involved in the praxis. Without risk there may be self-realization of some sort, but not the kind of change indicated by conscientization. For example, much of what passes for conscientization in the churches fails to make any significant change because it does not move beyond the safe harbors of verbosity and intellectualism. How many times have we tried to shock people into recognizing the suffering and pain which many people are forced to live with in this nation because of inadequate housing and employment? We may show films, pass out researched articles, hold forums, and even visit some pockets of poverty. Indeed, we might even succeed in raising the church's benevolence budget a few dollars. Yet it all eventually passes away until the next social issue is announced in the media. Throughout the ups and downs of our various campaigns, our lives and the church's structure remain the same. We want to raise our consciousness in the sense of being au courant, but we halt when this newly found knowledge begins to suggest that our lives might have to change if there is to be any change at all in the social problems we are studying.

Within this context, I remember a young man who spent a summer in a work camp in the South. Throughout the summer he lived and worked in a situation where he came face to face with the social problems of poverty that he had read about in his college textbooks. When he returned home to an affluent suburb, he found it quite difficult to adjust to his normal life. He was profoundly shaken by the extreme difference between his summer environment and the ambience of his comfortable home surroundings. He realized that the living room in his parents' house was almost twice as large as the small cabin he had shared with four other persons during the summer. He was shocked by the richness and careless abundance of the meals which his mother set before him. In beginning to deal with this situation, the young man reevaluated his former vocational plans and started to speak in terms of transferring to a college which would enable him to prepare for a medical career oriented to public health and rural medicine rather than the surgical specialization in a larger East Coast hospital he had always anticipated. At this point, his parents became quite concerned. Their son had gone too far. It was one thing to show concern for the less fortunate by spending a summer in volunteer service. But the thought of their son actually developing his future career around such concerns was beyond belief. Finally, the parents were able to convince their son that he needed professional help. They arranged for him to see a psychiatrist who gradually enabled the young man to work through this period of vocational uncertainty, to accept the limits of his situation, the romanticism of his ideals, and the futility of his dreams. In short, with professional assistance he was able to feel at home once again in his surroundings.

THE MILIEU AND MARX

Throughout the discussion of misappropriations of conscientization it has been apparent that Freire's pedagogy is dependent upon a rigorous cultural and class analysis. Freire insists that conscientization without class analysis is "small talk." "The prophetic position," Freire maintains, "demands a critical analysis of the social structures in which the conflict takes place. This means that it demands of its followers a knowledge of sociopolitical science, since this science cannot be neutral; this demands an ideological choice."[10] Freire's ideological choice, of course, is Marx. It is Marxist cultural and class analysis which he uses to prevent conscientization from becoming mythologized or methodized. Whenever Freire's praxis is discussed, there is usually great difference of opinion as to the extent of Marxist influence. It is clear, however, that critical awareness of class differentiation and its effects is a minimal requirement for anyone who would take Freire's pedagogy seriously.

The adoption of Marxist analysis constitutes a real problem for North Americans. One of the continuing themes in the history of American radicalism has been the periodic attempt to include our society within the eschatological scenario drawn up by the more doctrinaire Marxists. The procedure has failed as many times as it has been tried for the reason that the United States does not operate along the class lines envisioned by Marx. Our "proletariat" does not fit the Marxist model for revolution. Instead, the working class has been often one of the most ardent champions of capitalism. The tragedy of this history is that we have not developed genuine alternatives to the established social system. A resulting lack of forceful private counterpoints to the public sector has been the uncritical acceptance of such myths as "the middle class," the "melting pot," and "equal rights for all."

Pointing to the faults of Marxism, we have ignored the real lines of class division and cultural captivity which have become even more dominant in our denial of such phenomena. One very solid contribution that Freire makes to our situation is to underscore the importance of considering the social and class contexts of our lives. Unless transformation in the church is relegated to a false spirituality which denies the reality of our lives, it is impossible to deal with the full significance of faith without confronting the ways we are formed by these political and cultural factors. Too often our understanding of conversion has centered in privatistic models shaped by certain prototypes of conversion. When we think of conversion we almost automatically envision Paul being thrown off his horse on the road to Damascus, or Augustine telling all in his confessions, or John Wesley having his heart strangely warmed at Aldersgate. More often than not we refer to these persons to exemplify conversion, but in so doing we idealize the experience, sentimentalize its meaning, and push it further and further away from the central place it should occupy in the church. Focusing on the externals of these prototypical conversions, we lose sight of the center uniting the three, which is that all of them experienced a radically new understanding of themselves that was significantly different in each case, depending on the particular conditions of the individual's life. Freire reminds us that transformation occurs in the act of rethinking our lives, in the movement away from the general direction our lives have taken toward a reorientation in another way. Freire's work demonstrates the formative power of culture in shaping our perceptions and evaluations of the world. To speak of transformation in Christ and to see the church as a transforming community is at the least to take seriously the awesome task of becoming aware of our situation in life and the difficult process of changing our conditioned values, actions, and attitudes. Indeed, it is only by the grace of God that this act of re-creation emerges as a possibility in our lives.

CHAPTER SIX

TOWARD NEW OPTIONS

> Liberation is the presence of a new option, and only a non-conformed, covenanted people of God can offer that. Liberation is the pressure of the presence of a new alternative so valid, so coherent, that it can live without the props of power and against the stream of statesmanship. To be that option is to be free indeed.
>
> —John Howard Yoder[1]

If, as we have seen, the church has been tied uncritically to American popular culture; and if, as I have suggested, the church can change this situation only through the development of its critical consciousness, how then might our preceding discussion of Paulo Freire be relevant to the educational ministry of the church? I would maintain that his work urges us toward the consideration of issues and questions which can be the beginning of our own movement toward new options. In particular he pushes us toward a consideration of the paideia out of which our pedagogy proceeds.

The church as a community of integrity and transformation begins in recognition of its center. It is a community of faith insofar as it is faithful to its common tradition and the extent to which it articulates and enacts this memory as an event in this present moment. Memory in this sense is not a recital of past happenings, nor an individual act of remembering; rather, it is an encounter with a tradition of faith which has the power to transform and to be reinterpreted in the contemporary situation. The church should exist as a sign of the presence of God, the holy in the midst of life. Our concerns, structures, and vision should proceed from our understanding of this center rather than from our own accumulated opinions. This presumes, of course, that we know something about the content of this center of faith. It suggests that our primary concern should be the nature of our relationship to the holy rather than our collective goodwill to one another. We do not need the church as another excuse for simply getting together in fellowship. We do not need it as another institution for general education. And we have little reason for its existence as a partisan political caucus. We do need the church, however, as a witness to the transcendent and as a means to understand the end of all life. When the church forgets its mission as a sign of the holy, it loses its reason for being.

CHRISTIAN EDUCATION AS TRANSFORMATION

Christian education should focus on the responsibility of the faith community to communicate the gospel. It should cause those who seek liberation to remember the radical roots of the Christian faith. This communication of tradition is not simply instruction in the beliefs, practices, and stories of faith, it is also a dialogical, problem-posing process which frees the educator—and the student, as well—to experience the power of transformation in meeting Christ as the ultimate teacher in the church. In the end, learning is the achievement of the student, and in this sense faith begins with the person in relationship to God in the context of the faith community.

As I have tried to suggest in the preceding chapters, learning occurs by our participation in the communities to which we belong. The configuration of values, attitudes, and commitments—that is, the paideia—of the corporate life shapes our own perceptions and values. It forms our consciousness. This means that education to a large extent is our incorporation of the various models of identity which are available to us in a given social setting. In order to change or transform ourselves, then, there must be a new pattern, a reimaging of our conscious ideals, which occurs only through our participation in this new reality itself. In this way, conversion in the early church was understood as a long and careful process of introducing the convert to the beliefs and practices of the Christian community.

Transformation was not understood as a sudden and instant change of personality. Rather, it was acknowledged as a slow process of developing commitment. In the New Testament there is a continuing reference to the beginning of the Christian life as being similar to the experience of learning to walk. Yet this act of taking one's first steps in the way of Christ does not occur without the presence of others who are already walking in that way. The child, for example, must eventually act by himself, stand on his own two feet, but preparation for this task is a deliberate and sustained effort by adults to model the way of walking. If there were not others who could walk, it would be impossible for the child to understand the possibility of such an activity. The decision to become Christian is the decision to start walking in a certain direction toward a goal which reveals itself partially in the journey itself. The crude example of instantaneous conversion in the revival arena is far removed from the careful concern of the early Christians to understand transformation as a process rather than a magical moment. Neither is transformation in the Christian life simply the confirmation of the best values of the contemporary world. It is a new perception and a new belonging occasioned by encounter with a transcendent reality communicated by the community of faith but not possessed by it.[2]

However, even in this time of disestablishment and disillusionment with traditional religion, most people presume that they know what the gospel is about. The diffusion of the Christian faith in varying amounts throughout our culture promotes the impression that these remnant elements are the whole tradition. How many times have we heard it repeated that Christianity is the religion of the Golden Rule? Or how often have we seen the manners of the middle class become the Christian standard of the good life? A primary task of education in the liberal church has been to intensify this direction by trying to demythologize the gospel and make it relevant to the modern world. We have shifted our focus from the gospel to the world as the criterion of acceptability. The Christian faith, therefore, is judged acceptable by virtue of whether or not it fits the categories of the present age. Within this context, education becomes the apologetic task of finding ways to explain the gospel so that men and women can accept it. The educator becomes a propagandist and the church another marketplace for secular ideologies. The church continues to trivialize itself and to distort the gospel as it seeks to sell itself to the modern mind. Our current task is not so much that of modernizing the gospel as it is the effort to demythologize the modern mind itself. This is the thrust of Paul's letter to the Romans [12:2, NEB]: "Adapt yourself no longer to the pattern of this present world, but let your minds be remade and your whole nature thus transformed. Then you will be able to discern the will of God, and to know what is good, acceptable, and perfect."

The contemporary situation of education in the church is characterized by the fact that the church exists as only one of many institutions in society which barter for our loyalty. In a pluralistic society, identity is not so much inherited in tribal-like communities as it is determined by competition among various agencies. Unlike a tribe where identities are preconceived and to a certain extent prescribed by virtue of positions developed over many generations, our present world demands that we construct our individual identities within a varied set of alternative possibilities. One real problem with this process, of course, is the extent to which this personal development is a social construction of which we are relatively unconscious. We may not be aware of the choices we make; neither do we necessarily understand the multiple forces which influence our decisions. The choices we make, the identities we assume, may simply be the result of seductive, subliminal influences communicated by our cultural situation. We live within a time of curious paradox where we are superficially freed from the constraints of the tribal village, but we are tied even more narrowly to ideologies whose outlines we can only barely perceive.

Education as an act of cultural synthesis is the way in which we put together our individuality and family heritage with the various influences of the mass media, social groups, and historical moments which touch our lives. The crucial issue for Christian education is the relationship between the education communicated in the church and the deliberate as well as informal education which we all experience in the society at large. This means that a primary task of Christian education is to confront the syntheses already developed by persons in their experience in the world. We need to examine the content and outline of the learning which precedes and parallels our ongoing relationship with the church community. The difficulty in dealing with this question is the way in which we have been accustomed to affirming the values of American society as being synonymous with Christian values. Our familiar strategies, then, have been those of mutuality and support rather than critique and counterpoint.

THE CRITIQUE OF EVERYDAY LIFE

In suggesting that we need to address ourselves to the critical task of looking at the ideologies and values which shape us, I am not inferring that we simply suspend the task of critical thinking in regard to biblical interpretation. I am, though, maintaining that it is our secular fundamentalism—that is, our unconscious attachment to the mythologies of our culture—which needs to be dealt with in a sustained and critical way. This means that we must look at the world of everyday reality. We must help each other examine the thoughts and feelings which inform our perceptions and structure our actions. The problem is that this world of supermarkets, comic strips, *Time* magazine, and Saturday evening television shows is so much an accustomed part of our lives that we tend to diminish its significance in direct proportion to its presence in our lives. On the other hand, we have learned that popular culture is not to be taken with the same seriousness as the world of higher culture with its more sophisticated forms of art and entertainment. When the church, for example, organizes an adult study group, we generally gather people around the discussion of a current theological book or subject. We spend time with each other discussing a religious topic without ever dealing with the world of culture and reality which so fundamentally shapes our lives. What would it mean for us to reflect critically on the content of the television shows which take up so much of our time? What would we discover about the image of life conveyed by the currently popular situation comedies or variety shows? To what extent do these mass audience shows establish mythologies and fantasies which operate at the level of our unconscious? Do we vicariously participate in the antics of a television character or a professional football hero, or even the evening newscaster, to an extent which is more involving than any of the mystery cults and secret religions of the first century A.D.?

Within this context it is curious that television is so seldom used in adult education. We spend time and money locating and renting films for education programs, but we hardly ever think about using television itself as resource material. The reason for this neglect, I think, lies in the proximity that television has to our daily lives. It comes too close to home for comfort. As dramatic and personal as films can be, they still remain somewhat distant from our individual reality. Television shows, however, have become an accustomed part of our lives. Watching television with other people is similar to watching home movies together. It constitutes a sharing of our most private worlds.

It is this kind of replay of our personal worlds, however, which Paulo Freire evoked in the process of conscientization. Where Freire used photographs and tape recordings to play back cultural material to the groups of illiterate persons with whom he worked, so we can employ television programs in the same way. The network productions are collages of experience drawn from our culture and dramatized in almost archetypal forms. It becomes unclear, though, as to how much the culture influences the programs and vice versa. For many people, television characters and shows become as real as the human beings and situations which they meet in their lives. To a large extent we may prefer the electronic version to the real thing. The situation is close to that depicted in a cartoon: Two grandmotherly women are shown standing beside a baby carriage. One woman is pictured looking into the carriage and exclaiming, "You have a beautiful grandchild!" In reply, the other woman responds, "Oh, you haven't seen anything yet. Wait until I show you his photographs."

The afternoon soap operas, for example, might provide

another focus for conversations which would attempt to uncover the various levels of reality which they communicate. No one will admit they watch these programs, but someone out there is tuning in because they have some of the highest viewer ratings in the field. While I was pastor of a rural parish in New England I was perplexed at first about why it was that frequently when I called on families in the early afternoon the wives would excuse the absence of their husbands, maintaining they were busy. I knew the men were not in the milking barns, and I had never seen them on any other parts of the farm at this particular time either. In fact, I always tried to come at this hour because it was after lunch and before the late-afternoon milking. The matter was cleared up for me one day when the clerk at the general store told me it was at this time that "As the World Turns" and "Days of Our Lives" were telecast. As it turned out, all the men I had called on were devoted fans of these popular daytime dramas. I am not, of course, suggesting that the world would have been turned upside down for these men had I been able to meet with them and look at the images, icons, and ideas conveyed by these television series. But I would maintain that it is this kind of material that is a source of self-understandings and values for many persons. Neither individuals nor families can be fully conscious of the widely dispersed power of agencies in the media which we cannot see or effectively control. There is a danger of becoming a bit paranoid about the whole power of television, but it is difficult to exaggerate its importance as the most influential single factor in the emergence of the modern world. While we might have been concerned in an earlier time about the questionable influences existing outside the home in the form of peer groups, television has become so much a part of our families themselves that we find it almost impossible to differentiate ourselves from its influence.

The situation is particularly acute when we deal with the issue of the ideologies which influence the development of our children. The impact of television on child growth and development cannot be ignored. The average child, according to many of the reports issued in recent years, watches as many hours of television before he or she enters kindergarten as the average student will spend in getting a four-year B.A. degree in college. If the church means what it says about being a center of transformation, it must take seriously the agencies of conditioning in our society. One reason the Sunday school has become so identified with triviality and archaic knowledge is the way in which it perpetuates a world of unreality for children. We have held on to the Sunday school as a last refuge for the manners of the nineteenth century. The way we have dressed, talked, and acted on Sunday morning has conveyed a sense of being transported to another cultural era. The problem, of course, is that we have communicated the image of Jesus in the cultural patterns of a former time. We have tried to force children to read the Bible and to understand the story of Jesus in terms far removed from the cultural realities in which they find themselves. The situation, however, will be no better if we see our task as simply that of making the Sunday school a twentieth-century institution. The problem is more than that of updating the portrayals of Jesus from a nineteenth-century romantic figure to a mid-twentieth-century young rebel with a cause. The critical task begins when we see our responsibility toward children centering in helping them to develop a critical sense of the world and to cultivate the feelings and values suggested by the Christian faith.

One significant attempt at establishing this educational task is the work of the Education Center in St. Louis, Missouri. Under the leadership of Elsom Eldridge, the Center has developed curricula which help churches design educational programs aimed at crossing the boundary between religion and culture, between the Christian story and our own individual biographies. The model adopted by the Education Center is Jesus' use of stories dealing with the everyday reality of his own contemporaries. The center has developed courses which use children's literature itself as a vehicle for exploring the dimensions of being human. Such books as *The Velveteen Rabbit*, *Charlotte's Web*, and *The Secret Garden* evoke incisive questions about what it means to be human. They establish a point of contact between human events and experiences and the traditionally religious questions and answers. Moreover, they permit children and adults to join together in a common search for the elusive meanings of human valuing and acting. This approach does not imply a rejection of the Bible as a part of Christian education, but it does suggest that the biblical message, the Torah as a way of life, is best communicated by situating it in the midst of everyday life.

The concern, therefore, is to enable persons to confront the intersections in their lives where alternative decisions are possible and where the Christian tradition offers some ways of thinking and acting which bear on our decision-making. It does not really matter what the manifest nature of a certain curriculum or study group is all about because it is the presence or absence of this critical perspective which makes the difference. It is important, however, that we allow enough time for the kind of questioning and exploring necessary for dealing with the critical and constructive tasks as well. It may be that the traditional time limits of Sunday morning church schedules make this process impossible. We need to look into the use of other hours during the week and on weekends when we can set aside sufficient time to encourage group continuity and sustained inquiry.

AN ENDING AND SOME BEGINNINGS

I hope it is clear by now that what I am concerned about is the growth of an educational perspective in the church rather than the creation of new teaching and learning structures per se. The church already has a complicated series of educating occasions. The issue is the nature of the education which is being communicated by the existing reality of the institution. The educational task begins when we become critical of the values and meanings conveyed by these organizational realities and try to evoke alternative questions and concerns. Most certainly it indicates the rejection of education as a responsibility separate from the total life of the church. It means reconnecting the relationship between adults and children and emphasizing the networks of learning which include all ages. It demands that we see education within the larger context of the church's ministry and mission.

The church's ideal form is that of a covenant community, a people who share a common faith. Renewing the covenant, creating a sense of peoplehood, and striving to make the organization of the church itself a sign of hope are some of the various concerns which underlie our effort to evoke the church's growth as a liberating community and to encourage the development of its critical consciousness. The educational task begins with a group of people who take this responsibility seriously enough to initiate a conversation about its significance in their own community of faith. This group could be a board for Christian education, a diaconate, or any other committee of the church. It could be some parents along with other adults who want to examine the way the church is forming itself and informing the members of the church about the nature of the Christian faith. The beginning of educational inquiry in the church originates in the discovery of the continuing power of the Christian story as a means of empowerment for individual biographies. It continues as some group of persons in the church become clear about their objectives, formulate some methods for teaching and learning, and find some ways of evaluating what they are trying to do. But, most importantly, education emerges as an integral part of the church's ministry when we become aware of the possibilities of the church as a situation of response to God and a point of departure for understanding and transforming the personal and social contexts of our own lives.

A particular point at which education as transformation can begin in the church is the existing regularities of Sunday morning. First, we need to examine the nature of the service of worship from an educational perspective. What does the service itself look like? Do the setting and the feeling tone of the event convey a sense of transcendence, or do they simply reiterate the routines of any formal gathering? Who are the people present for worship? Is worship really an adult occasion, and, if this is our conclusion, what does this say about our rationalistic perceptions of faith itself? Does worship convey the sense of a community event, or is it just another of the endless consumer-oriented, self-improvement rituals? Ultimately I think we are brought back to the nature of liturgy and to a reevaluation of the meaning of worship. For too long, the free church tradition has been locked into formalized worship patterns that are far more inflexible than the most established liturgies of the Catholic tradition. Our freedom should allow us to explore a variety of liturgical possibilities rather than limiting us to either the arid intellectualism of a mythically inflated pulpit or the ersatz personalism of an ad lib celebrant.

Second, we need to take another look at the Sunday school as a means of Christian education. As I have tried to suggest, we ought to look at the continuation of this agency within the larger context of the church itself. In dealing with the Sunday school we have to be involved in an inquiry about the whole significance of Sunday morning as the primary occasion for the gathering of the church. We must examine the relationship between worship and education, the varied needs of the community, and the more specific purposes of the church as the body of Christ. Some parishes have moved to various adaptations of the traditional Sunday school and worship schedule. In many ways these recent innovations bring us back full circle to the nineteenth-century pattern of Sunday school followed by church, with plenty of time for conversation and socializing in between. But the importance of this development is the amount of time which the church spends in dealing with the reasons for either retaining or changing the Sunday morning patterns. Eventually, though, we will have to confront the latent issue of whether Sunday morning really is the most appropriate time for the main gatherings of the church. Perhaps worship, education, and fellowship should be situated during the week so as to leave the weekends for family events or more extended conferences and occasions for the church itself. It may be that the concentration of church life into one day has so emphasized the separation of religion from everyday life that it will only be by scheduling church worship throughout the week that we can even on a symbolic level suggest the interrelatedness of the sacred and the secular.

A third regularity of Sunday morning, a factor which is always present, is the minister himself or herself. It is the minister more than anyone else who communicates the spirit of the congregation. Although in the Protestant churches the minister's leadership is more persuasive than official, it nevertheless remains that he or she is the most influential figure in the congregation. Just as the church in general is searching for models and metaphors for itself, so is the minister in search of more adequate understandings of his/her ministry. The following words are a statement that a friend of mine read to his congregation in the hope that his sharing of his own personal struggle might enable them to join with him in a common pursuit of the meaning of the church itself.

> I do not know how it is where you work, but in the ministry I feel caught in the middle of everything that is happening today. It is very difficult to be a white Protestant minister today. For example, the black man says that I am a sellout to his people working a suburban church. The American Indian says that it is institutional Christianity that has contributed to the oppression of his people. The Jew tells me that I do not understand his feelings about the state of Israel. Students in our universities and colleges say that my profession continues an establishment that must go. The young in the church say that we are not communicating with them. Parents say that we have strayed too far from the teachings of the Bible. Liberals say that I drag my feet on social issues. Conservatives have even called me a Communist.

This minister went on to suggest that this personal situation was merely part of a larger pattern of difficulty which faced the whole congregation. He wondered aloud about the seriousness of persons' involvement in the church itself and whether there was anything more substantial to their life together than a series of itinerant meetings. He concluded by maintaining:

> I would like to say that more must be done here than re-deciding who will hand out the bulletins on Sunday morning and who will lead the Junior High youth group. These are symptoms of our problem and not the root cause of it. The problem is much deeper and much more complicated than that. What we must deal with is our commitment, our faith in God, and our desire to become a church.[3]

In the end, the congregation did try to look at itself as a community of faith and to discern the ways in which it could more fully express what it might mean to be a church. This return to some basic questions concerning the nature of the gospel raised for many people the fundamental issue as to whether they really did have any interest in the church apart from sheer habit and convention.

It seems to me that the kind of candor expressed by this minister, and his concern to direct this honesty toward the constructive task of inquiring into the reality of the church, suggests the emergence of education as a critical endeavor and the minister as a teacher. This minister urged the church to face the truth about itself, and in so doing he included himself as a part of the problem. He asked what difference it made for them to believe or not to believe, and he pushed them to inquire as to what this difference might mean in the structure of the congregation.

As we have seen in this example, the minister as teacher can emerge as the one who speaks with authority of his/her own struggle with the integrity of faith and the meaning of transformation in his/her own life. This means that the minister is not so much the one who knows but the one who is willing to teach and to learn as well, willing to explore the paideia of the Christian community and to search with others for styles of ministry appropriate and faithful in today's world. The minister is called to a congregation to initiate and to work with other Christians in the transformation of reality. The expectation that the church can become a community of faith may be an illusion, but it is the necessary illusion of those who have experienced the presence of God in their lives:

> But as for you, the initiation which you received from him stays with you; you need no other teacher, but learn all you need to know from his initiation, which is real and no illusion. As he taught you, then, dwell in him.
>
> —1 John 2:27, NEB

NOTES

PREFACE

1. Soren Kierkegaard, "Attack Upon 'Christendom,'" trans. by Walter Lowrie, in *A Kierkegaard Anthology,* ed. by Robert W. Bretall (Princeton: Princeton University Press, 1946), p. 448.

2. See Robert W. Lynn and Elliott Wright, *The Big Little School: Two Hundred Years of the Sunday School* (New York: Harper & Row, 1971).

3. Paul Tillich, *Theology of Culture,* ed. by Robert C. Kimball (New York: Oxford University Press, 1959), pp. 156-57.

CHAPTER ONE: THE DUBIOUS PARTNERSHIP

1. Brooks Atkinson, "A Puritan Boyhood," *The Massachusetts Review,* XV, 3 (Summer 1974), p. 373. Reprinted from *The Massachusetts Review.* © 1974 The Massachusetts Review, Inc. Used by permission.

2. Robert W. Lynn, *Protestant Strategies in Education* (New York: Association Press, 1964), p. 26.

3. Quoted in Peter Schrag, *The Decline of the WASP* (New York: Simon and Schuster, 1971), p. 20.

4. Ruth Miller Elson, *Guardians of Tradition: American Schoolbooks of the Nineteenth Century* (Lincoln: University of Nebraska Press, 1964), pp. 285, 337.

5. For an extended discussion of William H. McGuffey, see Robert W. Lynn, "Civil Catechetics in Mid-Victorian America:

Some Notes About American Civil Religion, Past and Present," *Religious Education,* LXVIII (Jan.-Feb. 1973), pp. 5-27.

6. Mark Twain, "The Story of the Good Little Boy," in *The Complete Short Stories of Mark Twain,* ed. by Charles Neider (New York: Bantam Books, 1957), pp. 66-70.

7. See Mark Sullivan, *Our Times* (New York: Charles Scribner's Sons, 1927), II, 23. In *The Christian Future* (New York: Harper & Bros., 1946), Eugen Rosenstock-Huessy commented on Dewey as the American Confucius; see pp. 43-53.

8. John Dewey, "The School and Society," in *Dewey on Education,* ed. by Martin S. Dworkin (New York: Teachers College, 1967), p. 49.

9. Ibid., p. 41.

10. John Dewey, "My Pedagogic Creed," in *Dewey on Education,* p. 32.

11. Quoted in Joel Spring, "Education as a Form of Social Control," in *Roots of Crisis: Essays in Twentieth Century Education,* ed. by Clarence J. Karrier and Paul C. Violas (Chicago: Rand McNally & Co., 1973), p. 31.

CHAPTER TWO: THE REVERENT SPECTATORS

1. Harvey Cox, *The Seduction of the Spirit* (New York: Simon and Schuster, 1973), p. 52.

2. Quoted in Bruce Mazlish, *In Search of Nixon* (New York: Basic Books, 1972), p. 53.

3. Brooks Atkinson, "A Puritan Boyhood," *The Massachusetts Review,* XV, 3 (Summer 1974), p. 339. Reprinted from *The Massachusetts Review.* © 1974 The Massachusetts Review, Inc. Used by permission.

4. Ibid.

5. John Updike, "Museums and Women," in *Museums and Women* (New York: Fawcett World Library, 1973), p. 16.

Copyright © 1960, 1965, 1966, 1967, 1968, 1969, 1970, 1971, 1972 by John Updike. Used by permission of Alfred A. Knopf, Inc.

6. John Updike, "The Deacon," in *Museums and Women*, p. 40.

7. Ibid., pp. 42-43.

8. Ibid., p. 45.

9. Ibid., p. 46.

10. Peter Berger, et al., *The Homeless Mind* (New York: Random House [Vintage Books], 1974), p. 184.

11. Dean M. Kelley, *Why Conservative Churches Are Growing* (New York: Harper & Row, 1972), p. 35.

12. See *The Wall Street Journal*, January 11, 1973, pp. 1, 20.

13. John Updike, "The Deacon," pp. 45-46.

CHAPTER THREE: CONNECTIONS

1. Bernard Meland, *Faith and Culture* (London: George Allen and Unwin Ltd., 1955), p. 21.

2. The thoughts of this chapter are indebted to the stimulating article written by Herbert W. Richardson, "Three Myths of Transcendence," which was included in *Transcendence*, ed. by Herbert W. Richardson and Donald R. Cutler (Boston: Beacon Press, 1969), pp. 98-113.

3. John Henry Newman, "Lead, Kindly Light" (1833), in *The Hymnal of the United Church of Christ* (Philadelphia: United Church Press, 1974), p. 292.

4. Sabine Baring-Gould, "Onward, Christian Soldiers" (1864), in *The Hymnal of the United Church of Christ*, p. 205.

5. Norman Mailer, *The Armies of the Night* (New York: Signet Books, 1968), p. 320.

6. Herbert W. Richardson, "Three Myths of Transcendence," in *Transcendence*, pp. 111-12.

7. Quoted in Robert E. Ornstein, *The Psychology of Consciousness* (San Francisco: W. H. Freeman and Co., 1972), p. 187.

CHAPTER FOUR: CONTEXTS

1. C. Ellis Nelson, *Where Faith Begins* (Richmond: John Knox Press, 1967), pp. 10, 186.

2. Soren Kierkegaard, "Armed Neutrality," in *Armed Neutrality and an Open Letter,* ed. and trans. by Howard V. Hong and Edna H. Hong (New York: Simon and Schuster, 1969), p. 34.

3. John B. Cobb, Jr., *Liberal Christianity at the Crossroads* (Philadelphia: Westminster Press, 1973), p. 12.

4. See C. Ellis Nelson, *Where Faith Begins;* "Is Christian Education Something Particular?" *Religious Education,* LXVII (Jan.-Feb. 1972), pp. 5-15; John H. Westerhoff III and Gwen Kennedy Neville, *Generation to Generation* (Philadelphia: United Church Press, 1974).

5. See Werner Jaeger, *Paideia: The Ideals of Greek Culture* (New York: Oxford University Press, 1945), and Charles R. Stinnette, Jr., *Learning in Theological Perspective* (New York: Association Press, 1965).

CHAPTER FIVE: CONSCIOUSNESS

1. James Agee, *Let Us Now Praise Famous Men* (Boston: Houghton Mifflin Co., 1939), p. 307.

2. Eugen Rosenstock-Huessy, *I Am an Impure Thinker* (Norwich, Vt.: Argo Books, 1970), p. 189.

3. See Paulo Freire, *The Pedagogy of the Oppressed* (New York: Herder & Herder, 1970); *Education for Critical Consciousness* (New York: Seabury Press, 1974); "Education, Liberation, and the Church," *Study Encounter,* IX, 1 (1973), pp. 1-16. See also, "Education for Awareness: A Talk with Paulo Freire," *Risk,* VI, 6 (1970), pp. 7-17.

4. Quoted in James A. Farmer, Jr., "Adult Education for Transiting," in *Paulo Freire: A Revolutionary Dilemma for the Adult Educator,* ed. by Stanley M. Grabowski (Syracuse, N.Y.: Publications in Continuing Education, 1972), p. 1. Used by permission of James A. Farmer, Jr.

5. See Paulo Freire, "Education, Liberation, and the Church."

6. Quoted in Kathy Kahn, *Hillbilly Women* (New York: Avon Books, 1972), pp. 115-16. Copyright © 1972, 1973 by Kathy Kahn. Used by permission of Doubleday & Company, Inc.

7. Charles Reich, *The Greening of America* (New York: Random House, 1970), p. 19.

8. Ibid., p. 18.

9. Paulo Freire, "Education, Liberation, and the Church," p. 3.

10. Ibid., p. 14.

CHAPTER SIX: TOWARD NEW OPTIONS

1. John Howard Yoder, "Exodus and Exile: Two Faces of Liberation," *Cross Currents,* XXIII, 3 (Fall 1973), p. 309.

2. For an excellent discussion of education in the New Testament see Ian A. Muirhead, *Education in the New Testament* (New York: Association Press, 1965).

3. A statement read by the Rev. Archie D. McRee, a minister in the Massachusetts Conference of the United Church of Christ. Reprinted by permission.

ABOUT THE AUTHOR

Malcolm L. Warford, a native of Lexington, Kentucky, is a graduate of Transylvania College (B.A.), Andover Newton Theological School (B.D.), and Columbia University (Ed.D.). After receiving the Page Graduate Fellowship, he did graduate study in the history of religions at McGill University.

Dr. Warford is an ordained minister of the United Church of Christ and has served churches in Strafford, Vermont and Scarsdale, New York. Prior to entering the ministry he was a teacher in an inner-city school of Cincinnati, Ohio. He has been a member of the executive committee of the Association of Professors and Researchers in Religious Education, and he is currently part of the resource team for Ministries in Public Education. Holding membership in various theological and educational societies, the author has published articles on education and Christian education, cultural action and change.

From 1972 to 1976, Dr. Warford was assistant professor of theological studies at St. Louis University; director of the university's A.M. degree in religion and education; and a member of the core faculty of the Man, Technology, and Society program in the college of arts and sciences. He is now director of educational research and associate professor of religion and education at Union Theological Seminary in New York City.

Malcolm L. Warford is director of educationul research and associate professor of religion and education at Union Theological Seminary in New York City. From 1972 to 1976, he was assistant professor of theological studies at St. Louis University; director of the university's A.M. degree in religion and education; and a member of the core faculty of the Man, Technology, and Society program in the college of arts and sciences. He is a graduate of Transylvania College (B.A.), Andover Newton Theological School (B.D.), and Columbia University (Ed.D.); he has also done graduate study in the history of religions at McGill University.

Dr. Warford is an ordained minister of the United Church of Christ and has pastored churches in Strafford, Vermont and Scarsdale, New York. Prior to entering the ministry he was a teacher in an inner-city school of Cincinnati, Ohio. Dr. Warford has been a member of the executive committee of the Association of Professors and Researchers in Religious Education, and he is currently part of the resource team for Ministries in Public Education. He holds membership in various theological and educational societies.

A leader of workshops and seminars for local churches, ministers' groups, religious orders, and religion teachers, Malcolm Warford has published articles, in a number of journals, on education and Christian education, cultural action and change.